Wellington Koo

Makers
of the
Modern
World

Wellington Koo
China
Jonathan Clements

HH
HAUS HISTORIES

First published in Great Britain in 2008 by
Haus Publishing Ltd
26 Cadogan Court
Draycott Avenue
London SW3 3BX
www.hauspublishing.com

A CIP catalogue record for this book
is available from the British Library

ISBN 978-1-905791-69-9

Series design by Susan Buchanan
Typeset in Sabon by MacGuru Ltd
Printed in Dubai by Oriental Press
Maps by Martin Lubikowski, ML Design, London

Contents

For Aaron Sorkin
'Decisions are made by those who show up.'

Note on names

Names in this book reflect current usage, not the variant spellings utilised in 1919, Hepburn romanisation for Japanese and Pinyin for Chinese – hence Lu Zhengxiang instead of Lou Tseng-Tsiang, Beijing not Peking, and Shandong not Shantung. The book retains Western names where Chinese use them in dealings with foreigners, hence Wellington Koo, not Gu Weijun (in Pinyin romanisation), or Ku Wei-chun (in Wade-Giles romanisation). Overseas Chinese who use a non-Mandarin dialect are called by their preferred romanisation with a Mandarin gloss where known, hence Oei Hui-lan. Beijing was renamed Beiping (Peiping) during the period when Nanjing (Nanking) was China's capital, but is referred to as Beijing throughout to avoid confusion.

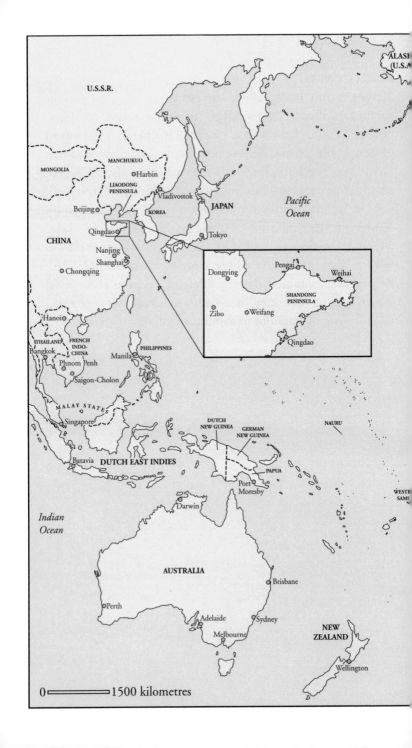

Introduction

Stephen Bonsal, secretary to the American diplomat Colonel Edward House at the Paris Peace Conference, had every sympathy for the Chinese delegation, if not for their putative leader. He confided to his diary, a work not published until a generation later, that he had 'no confidence' in the integrity of the leading Chinese delegate, Lu Zhengxiang – a man whom he suspected of taking bribes during the Boxer Rebellion negotiations of 1900, and whom he all but accused of being a Japanese patsy at the Peace Conference.

'It is a thousand pities that Wellington Koo and Alfred Sze are not the leading delegates of China here,' wrote Bonsal.[1] Like many of the delegates, he had been deeply impressed by the dashing young Wellington Koo, an American-educated ambassador whose mastery of debate and diplomacy had charmed the Council.

Quite by accident, Bonsal was to get his wish. The Chinese delegation did not represent a unified nation, and conflict among its members was to push aside its supposed leader. Even the argumentative Chinese delegates could see that Wellington Koo, a former Chinese minister in Washington, enjoyed a special relationship with Woodrow Wilson – they had even arrived in Europe on the same ship. With Lu Zheng-xiang failing to achieve much of merit, Koo was pushed into the limelight, firstly as a prominent speaker, and then as the delegation's official spokesman.

The Chinese homeland was already carved up between numerous interest groups: republicans, rival warlords claiming to be old-school monarchists, and a dozen European powers intent on clinging to colonial concessions on Chinese territory. China risked complete collapse, and its delegates represented two rival governments. Koo, based in Beijing and famous for refusing to take sides in local conflicts, rose above factionalism to plead China's case, particularly in the controversial topic of the Shandong Peninsula.

Perilously close to Beijing, and with a population, area and natural resources easily the match of a major European power, Shandong was a ready-made princedom. The ancient birthplace of Confucius himself, a fact that Koo slyly parsed with emotive language as 'China's Holy Land', it had been a German colony until wrested from its occupiers by the Japanese. Now, in the aftermath of the First World War, the question remained: to whom should Shandong be restored? The Germans had been railroaded into giving up all territorial claims beyond continental Europe, but the Japanese claimed to have received wartime promises that Shandong was theirs for the taking.

Shandong was one of the hottest topics in Paris. Radical Chinese students threatened to break up any public discussion with demonstrations of their own. An ill-advised smear campaign against the Japanese filled the press with stories (many of them true) of atrocities committed against civilisation itself by these supposed allies of the Great Powers, with China as the victim. As the Conference went on and the

Shandong debates appeared to favour Japan, America got the blame, since many Chinese felt that Woodrow Wilson had broken a promise.

Wilson had looked the Chinese in the eye and said: 'You can rely on me.'

We did, complained Koo to his adviser, *and now we are betrayed in the house of our only friend.*[2]

In early May, Koo paid a personal call on Colonel House at the American headquarters, where he played the last of his dwindling cards. He revealed that the conditions of the Peace Conference were veering so far away from China's interests, that he was seriously considering not signing the Treaty of Versailles at all. The threat of non-signature, when wielded by the Japanese, had been sufficient to sway many concessions in their favour; but with an ineffective and weak nation, ironically regarded as one of the 'small' countries participating, Koo did not enjoy the same power.

If Peking orders me to sign the treaty, he said, *I will sign – otherwise not.*

Colonel House tried to cheer him up. The Japanese were sure to move out of Shandong, he said. The League of Nations would make sure of it, and when that inevitably happened, Koo would be seen as the hero of the hour.

But I'll be a dead hero, Koo replied. *If I sign the treaty – even under orders from Peking – I shall not have what you in New York call a Chinaman's chance.*

Koo genuinely feared for his life, for what might be done to him by Chinese radicals if he let his country down before the watching world.

I am too young to die, he said as he left. *I hope they will not make me sign. It would be my death sentence.*

∞∞∞

Wellington Koo (1888–1985) was born and raised in Shang-hai's International Settlement, a foreign enclave in which the Chinese themselves were regarded as second-class citizens. He experienced first-hand the injustices of China's 'Unequal Treaties' with foreign powers, and was one of the handful of young scholars in whom late imperial China invested all its progressive hopes.

By the time Koo was recalled to his homeland in 1912, after his studies in America, a newly acquired doctorate of law in hand, the imperial system had been swept away and replaced with a chaotic, corrupt series of bickering republicans, grasp-ing warlords and embittered restorationists. Koo was sent abroad again as China's minister to Washington, where he fostered a respectful relationship with the American Presi-dent, Woodrow Wilson. At the close of the First World War, he was one of the bright intellectuals sent to plead China's case before the Paris Peace Conference. While most countries had sent their elder statesmen and great diplomats, many of the Chinese delegation were a full generation younger than those from the Great Powers. Moreover, they were a squab-bling cabal that reflected the lack of unified government back home. Thrust into the limelight by his personal connections with Wilson and by internal disputes among the Chinese, Koo became his country's most outspoken and eloquent cham-pion at the Paris Peace Conference.

While Paris was a swan-song for many careers, Koo's was only just beginning. It also saw his attempt to rebuild a shat-tered personal life. Newly widowed by the influenza pan-demic of 1918, Koo's sojourn in Paris saw his whistle-stop pursuit of and betrothal to the woman who would become his third wife, the sugar-cane heiress Oei Hui-lan. The 32-year-old diplomat made his maiden speech *at* the Conference, initiating three further decades in politics that would see him briefly appointed President of China, before serving in further diplomatic posts in Britain, France, Mexico and the United States.

A hero to the Chinese, Koo was also a creature of contradictions. He was a career diplomat whose country was in chaos – at Versailles, he was obliged to juggle his mission with conflicting orders from two opposing regimes. He was an advocate for clear and transparent government, and yet is often believed to have been responsible for several wily press leaks that placed an unwelcome pressure on his rivals at Paris. He remained dutifully loyal to the government of north China, even when its popular support fell apart and power reverted to unelected dictators. He was a staunch supporter of China as a modern republic, but also of Yuan Shikai, the warlord who would attempt to proclaim himself a new emperor. Declared a criminal in the 1920s by Chiang Kai-shek's Guomindang government, Koo would eventually rise to become Chiang's special adviser on foreign policy – his career salvaged by the intercession of another warlord, the 'Young Marshal' Zhang Xueliang. Koo was immensely popular with the foreign ambassadorial community, but some critics regarded him as *too* American in his attitude and behaviour – ironically, some regarded him as not Chinese enough. He argued passionately and powerfully for China to be recognised as a modern, civilised state, but did so in the expectation that his radical countrymen would murder him if he offered concessions. He was a valiant opponent of inequities in China, particularly extraterritoriality and foreign occupation, but probably saved his own life by seeking asylum with the British in Weihaiwei

– a colony whose presence he had previously tried to abolish. In 1999, long after his death, his role at the Paris Peace Conference became the subject of an adoring Chinese movie, *My 1919*, in which Koo was portrayed by the actor Chen Daoming as a people's hero, not just to the Nationalists that he represented, but to all of China, including the Communist successors he had himself repudiated.

History dealt Koo an unfair hand. Despite his supreme talents and tireless labours, he was rarely able to put his skills to use from a superior or even level position. He spent his entire diplomatic life on damage control, and the Paris Peace Conference was no exception. Koo was tasked with extricating China from unequal treaties made with foreign powers, particularly Japan, although he arrived in Paris fully aware that China had already signed a secret treaty under duress to honour Japan's gains. Koo knew this better than most, since he had drafted its wording himself from a hospital bed in Beijing.

Despite infamously refusing to sign the Treaty of Versailles, Koo was afforded a better opportunity than any other delegate to participate in its legacy. He was present at many of the subsequent conferences that attempted to keep peace alive, including that in Washington from 1921–2, at which he successfully engineered the Nine Power Treaty – a document that helped undo, at least on paper, some of the injustices of Versailles. When this, too, failed to halt Japan's Chinese land-grab, Koo was a reluctant member of the ill-fated Lytton Commission that tried and failed to enforce the mandate of the League of Nations in Japanese-occupied Manchuria. It was also his stirring speech in Geneva that immediately preceded the momentous walkout by the Japanese delegates in 1933. Not only did Koo have a ringside seat for the rise and fall of the League of Nations, as a founder member of the League's successor, Koo was instrumental in preserving the position of Republican China, now confined to the small island of Taiwan, on the United Nations Security Council. By 1949, the Communists proclaimed themselves to be the new rulers of China itself. Retiring from the diplomatic service in 1956, the venerable Koo went on to become a judge at the International Court of Justice at The Hague, rising to vice-president before his second retirement, aged 79, in 1967.

He settled in New York, where his twilight years were haunted by the decline in influence of 'Republican' China – he lived to see the loss of China's seat on the Security Council to the Communists, but died two years before four decades of martial law was finally lifted in Taiwan.

Wellington Koo, the Chinese Nationalist envoy, photographed at the Overseas Press Club in Washington DC. February 1955

I
The Life and the Land

1

The Unequal Treaties

For decades, explorers and traders had travelled further eastward across Siberia. Russia, still nominally a European power, swiftly laid claim to vast tracts of Asia. By the late 17th century, the domain claimed by the Tsar had bumped into the northern reaches of the domain claimed by the Chinese Emperor. After initial clashes, a common border was agreed, and the possibilities for trade discussed. Imperial China, however, was not really interested. It had long prided itself on its lack of necessity for foreign goods, and long cherished the belief that it sat at the centre of the world, and that its ruler, the Emperor, was the lord of all under heaven.

Events at the borders suggested otherwise, but the Emperor was far away, mired in a bureaucracy of pomp and ceremony that offered no clue that the world was changing. And yet, even in the 17th century, foreign 'barbarians' began to contend over Chinese resources. The Dutch and Portuguese squabbled over Macao; the English, Dutch and Spanish over Taiwan.

For centuries, China had been able to maintain the illusion of being aloof from the rest of the world. The overland road from Europe was littered with dangers, searing deserts and freezing mountain peaks. The sea route took months, and was no less hazardous.

Modern technology brought China within reach. It was Great Britain in the 18th century, with its thirst for tea in porcelain ('china') cups, and its love of silk, that was first to notice a serious trade deficit. The Chinese were selling the British what they wanted, but the British had nothing to offer the Chinese in return. To Britain's eternal shame, it found a commodity that would help balance things. Crops of the deadly, addictive opium poppy were harvested in British India and offloaded on the southern Chinese. Opium was illegal in China and its trade not authorised by the British Crown, yet nevertheless the ships that arrived to buy tea did so with holds full of opium.

> Taiwan is a large island off the south-west coast of China, once a base for pirates. It was occupied by the Qing dynasty in the late 17th century in order to put down a resistance movement of loyalists to the deposed Ming regime, but remained peripheral to Chinese interests. There were several attempts by the Japanese to invade, occupy or purchase Taiwan in the late 19th century, and it was eventually seized as a spoil of war in 1895. The island remained in Japanese hands until 1945.

The East India Company, the venture that had pioneered the peddling of drugs to the Chinese, lost its monopoly on the Far East trade in 1834. In the interests of protecting legitimate merchants from pirates, brigands and other menaces, the Royal Navy began to make its presence felt in the Far East.

In 1839, the Chinese commissioner Lin Zexu ordered a trade embargo against the British. He rounded up all the opium in Canton and destroyed it. Many British merchants were made to sign an undertaking not to sell drugs to the Chinese again, and Lin took the remarkable step of writing directly to Queen Victoria to explain his actions. His communiqué, which may have never reached the monarch to whom it was addressed, noted that Her Majesty should consider herself notified of what some of her subjects had been doing in her name, and of the Chinese intention not to tolerate it.

Britain's response was military. In 1840, the Royal Navy steamed into Chinese waters, supposedly to avenge the destruction of British subjects' property. Warships packing powerful guns and highly-trained marines made short work of China's outmoded coastal defences, advancing up the coast, past what was then the small village of Shanghai, and seizing control of the Yangtze River, a vital conduit into China's heart.

This First Opium War ended with the Treaty of Nanjing in 1842, in which the Chinese promised to pay compensation for the opium Lin had destroyed, and reparations for the cost incurred by the British in waging war against them. Several treaty ports were to be opened on the Chinese coast to afford British merchants better access to their markets and most notoriously, the obscure offshore island of Hong Kong was to become a British possession, so that British ships could enjoy access to a permanent harbour. Moreover, the Chinese were forced to agree not to impose their own justice on British nationals on their territory. Instead, henceforth, the British would enjoy 'extraterritoriality' – the right to live under their own laws, and to be tried by their own courts, even for crimes committed on Chinese soil.

This was only the first of the Unequal Treaties to be imposed upon the Chinese in the 19th century. Soon other countries, France, then the young United States, then Prussia and Germany, concluded similar deals, often after similar bouts of gunboat diplomacy. Further foreign concessions were carved out of Chinese territory, with some treaty 'ports' now found far inland, at railheads and on riverbanks, where the Chinese were no longer masters of their own country. Unequal Treaties opened the door for Christian missionaries, allowed to preach their foreign religion on Chinese soil, and protected by extraterritoriality from any protests to the contrary.

China lost control of its own tax revenues, with import tariffs now imposed and collected by the treaty port owners. In a final insult, the Treaty of Nanjing and its imitators inserted a clause for 'Most Favoured Nation' status into its wording, ensuring that any advantages secured with one nation would benefit all the others. Thus, French gains in a particular treaty port would automatically apply to all other powers, while, for example, a preferential tax rate offered to Germans would similarly apply to all foreigners. It gave the impression that all Western Powers were united in a mission to exploit China, driving their wedges of control ever deeper into Chinese sovereignty while the emperors struggled to maintain their authority.

The Second Opium War of 1856–60 showed the foreign powers at work. Chinese officials boarded a Chinese smuggling vessel, the *Arrow*, which had been registered in Hong Kong, and was hence technically a 'British' ship. Using this flimsy pretext as a means to demand better terms for the old Treaty of Nanjing, British gunboats descended upon Canton. Soon after, the French joined in, ostensibly to avenge the murder of a French missionary. A joint Anglo-French force captured the Dagu forts near Tianjin, and, after news arrived of the torture and execution of some European prisoners of war, destroyed the priceless Summer Palace in revenge.

As a result of the Second Opium War, Britain and her allies, and hence all foreign powers under the terms of Most Favoured Nation status, gained the right to station foreign legations in Beijing, the sacred imperial capital, within a stone's-throw of the Emperor. There were further indemnities to be paid, opium was now legalised, and further lands on the border of Hong Kong handed over to the British.

The Chinese acquiesced in part because they had other problems: natural disasters, a Muslim secessionist movement in the western hinterland, and a catastrophic insurrection in the Yangtze region that lasted for 14 years. The Taiping Rebellion was formed from a fatal cocktail of China's 19th century ills. Its leader, Hong Xiuquan, had repeatedly failed the Chinese civil service examinations, intricate contests in poetry and literary criticism that were mandatory for anyone seeking a post in the Chinese government. After yet another letdown in the pointless exams, Hong reputedly had a vision, inspired by some missionary pamphlets he had read, telling him that he was the son of the Christian God, and fated to become a new emperor. The subsequent religious-military movement Hong unleashed is remembered as a rebellion, but is perhaps better classified as the Taiping 'War', with estimates of the death toll running as high as 20 million. The Taiping advance was only halted by foreign intervention, when a mercenary force out of Shanghai, trained by Western officers, joined with the beleaguered imperial army to stop them.

Shanghai soon grew into an exclusive foreign city on Chinese territory. The Chinese districts of the city remained much as they had before, with some parts left in ruins by the years of warfare. The foreign enclave became one of the most modern cities in the world, with trams and electric streetlights. Shanghai was particularly favoured by Germany, whose bankers funnelled investment into the region, using the city as a base. The American and British concessions soon grew so large that they joined to form a single International Settlement. The French, for their part, refused to join the new foreign-run Shanghai Municipal Council, and formed their own French settlement in another part of the city.

Shanghai and its environs was a boomtown for foreign interests, and indeed offered opportunities for many Chinese. For its residents, however, the city also offered a first-hand view of the injustices of the Unequal Treaties. Parts of the International Settlement operated under a form of Asian *apartheid*, with parks forbidden to Chinese, and a police force officered by foreigners.

ooooo

Wellington Koo was born on 29 January 1888, in Shanghai. As this is often listed in a Chinese fashion as the 17th day of the 12th lunar month, it is sometimes assumed that he was born in 1887. His Chinese name was Gu Weijun, often romanised as Ku Wei-chün. His own preferred romanisation was Koo Vi Kyuin, hence the customary appearance of his name as V K Wellington Koo.

The Gu family came from Hunan province, higher up the Yangtze River, and had moved downstream in the 17th century. For much of the ensuing Qing dynasty, the family dwelled at Jiading in Jiangsu province, about an hour upriver from the growing metropolis of Shanghai – a century later, Jiading is now contained within the city limits.

The Gu clan were merchants, although they sent many sons to sit the civil service exams. During the Qing dynasty, many Gu men passed the local equivalent of bachelor's or master's degrees, and some went on to work in the government. Wellington's father had arrived in Shanghai as an infant refugee during the Taiping Rebellion. Grandmother Gu had fled the troubles with her two young children, and made a precarious living as a seamstress.

Wellington's father, Gu Rong, became an apprentice at a Shanghai customs brokerage aged just 13, and by 16 he was married, to Wellington's mother Jiang Fu-an. Fu-an was a traditional Chinese wife, her feet bound in the crippling affectation that was supposed to render a woman's gait attractively delicate. She ruled all within the home, but only ventured beyond it in the summer, when she would travel upriver to visit relatives. Gu Rong prospered in business, setting up the Shen Yu Hang hardware store on Shanghai's Fuzhou Road, and soon growing wealthy on the eternal demand for new inventions and implements.

In later life, Gu Rong took on government contracts as an excise man, and often travelled deep into the hinterland. 'There were no railroads in those days,' wrote his daughter-in-law, 'and his rounds were made in slow tempo, astride a donkey, or by sedan chair. With him went the money bags heavy with silver levied by the emperor's faraway magistrates.'[1] By the end of his career, Gu Rong had risen from shopkeeper to President of the Bank of Communications.

Wellington Koo had been a sickly child, and family legend maintained that he had nearly died as an infant, until a Chinese doctor cured him. The grateful Gu Rong had rashly promised Doctor Zhang that his efforts would be rewarded a thousandfold, and that when young Wellington was fully-grown, he would marry the doctor's daughter.[2]

Gu Rong's properties included houses in Jiading and in nearby Suzhou, and a family home in the International Settlement. All of this, it was expected, would eventually pass to the eldest son, raised in the Confucian tradition, but Gu Rong was determined that his two other boys would excel in different areas. What we might call Wellington's primary school education was conducted in a typical Confucian style, learning to read by rote from the same books that had been used for centuries in China. Wellington's teacher was a Master Zhu, the holder of a bachelor's degree whose failure to secure a master's had kept him in the provinces as a schoolteacher.

But although his mentor instilled a Confucian sense of propriety in the young Koo, times were changing. Koo's time at Master Zhu's academy was concurrent with the embarrassing defeat of the imperial forces in the Sino-Japanese War.

Nominally still a tributary state to the Chinese emperor, Korea had steadily fallen under Japanese influence during the late 19th century. Unlike the Western Powers squabbling over other parts of Chinese territory, Japan's interests in Korea were not merely commercial. There were also strategic concerns: Korea was the closest point on the Asian mainland to Japan, and was the obvious point from which a belligerent force might launch an attack on the Japanese islands. The chances of China doing so were remote indeed, but military thinking in Tokyo still regarded Korea as a 'dagger pointed at the heart of Japan' – a phrase occasionally ascribed to Tokyo's Prussian military advisers, and sometimes to Japanese leaders.

Under the Convention of Tianjin of 1885, China and Japan were obliged to notify each other of any plan to send troops into Korea. Each side, however, interpreted this differently. The Japanese saw it as an agreement not to get involved in Korean matters, at least not officially. The Chinese saw it as a simple requirement to keep the Japanese apprised of troop movements. When the Chinese sent troops in to Korea to suppress a conservative, anti-foreign rebellion, the Japanese responded in kind, sending a considerably larger retaliatory force.

China's military forces had been trapped in separate, segregated battalions since the upheavals of the Taiping Rebellion – often divided on regional or racial lines. The Beiyang or 'North Sea' forces of the Beijing area were thus left to deal with the Japanese incursions almost single-handedly. Although the Chinese possessed a few modern ships, often commanded by American or European officers, they were little match for the Japanese navy.

The conflict in Korea soon spilled across the Yalu River into Manchuria and China. In the humiliating Treaty of Shimonoseki of 1895, China was forced to pay an indemnity to Japan, cede Korea to Japanese influence, along with the southern island of Taiwan, and, initially, the strategically important Liaodong Peninsula. To add insult to injury, Liaodong was only returned to Chinese hands through threats issued by other foreigners – Russia, France and Germany initiating a 'Triple Intervention' designed to prevent the Japanese from reaping the full benefits of their military gains.

Although the Triple Intervention was an annoyance to the Japanese, it made little difference in China, and only emphasised the situation – China's wishes on its own territory were largely ignored in favour of the arguments of foreign powers. For Gu Rong and his family, the most immediate effect was to be seen on the Yangtze River itself, where Japanese gunboats were permitted to join the foreign ships sailing past Shanghai and deep into Chinese territory.

Although Wellington Koo was only a child at the time, he remembered the Japanese victory for the rest of his life. *Ever since I was seven years old*, he wrote, *when I heard with depressed heart the news of China's defeat by Japan, I had desired to work for China's recovery and the removal of the Japanese menace.*[3]

Gu Rong was counted among the many Chinese who held China's traditions, stultifying and ossified, to be at least partly responsible for the ignominious defeat. Although China had made occasional efforts to modernise, Japan had embraced new technology with gusto. The Japanese navy, with steam ships and modern guns, had wiped out a poorly funded, outmoded Chinese force that even included wooden junks. Positions of authority in the Chinese government required the regurgitation of knowledge in exams whose contents had remained unchanged for literally centuries. The Chinese education system was state-of-the-art for 1400 AD, but less useful in a modern world that valued science and technology. Japan had a modern shipping fleet, railways and factories; Tokyo was mounting an effective resistance to foreign imperialists, and even asserting control over her Chinese neighbours. The Sino-Japanese War was an intense embarrassment, and even if the declining Qing dynasty was unable to act on the signs, some of the foreign powers certainly would.

> **Ever since I was seven years old, when I heard with depressed heart the news of China's defeat by Japan, I had desired to work for China's recovery and the removal of the Japanese menace.**
> **WELLINGTON KOO**

Germany, in particular, had been eyeing eastern China for over a decade, ever since the traveller Ferdinand von Richthofen, uncle of the more famous 'Red Baron', had toured the province in the 1870s. An acknowledged China expert, and the man who coined the term 'Silk Road', Richthofen had reported to the Kaiser that Shandong's Jiaozhou Bay was the finest harbour in all Asia. In 1896, the commander of

Germany's East Asia Squadron, Admiral Tirpitz, examined the bay himself, and confirmed that it was an ideal site for a naval base.

Shandong, however, was also a lawless and dangerous territory, and had been ever since the upheavals of the Sino-Japanese War. The Big Sword Society, a semi-religious group of revolutionaries, fiercely contested all foreign influence, including the Society of the Divine Word, a German Catholic missionary organisation that had arrived in 1882 to propagate the Gospel. On 1 November 1897, a group of Big Sword soldiers were sent to assassinate a German priest. Not finding him at home, they instead brutally hacked to death two other German missionaries.

Kaiser Wilhelm II called the incident 'a splendid opportunity' – his order to retaliate reached the East Asia Squadron within a week.[4] On 14 November, German troops poured onto the beaches at Jiaozhou, while the Beijing government feebly protested. Within three months, the incident had been 'settled' with the granting of a 99-year lease to Germany for the strategic bay, and its nearby port of Qingdao. But Germany also gained a hold over the rest of the peninsula, with railway concessions, mining rights and permission to station troops in the hinterland for the 'protection' of its subjects. It was yet another concession to the grasping foreign powers, but Shandong would prove to be particularly important to Wellington Koo, at the time still a boy of only nine.

At 11 years of age, Wellington was enrolled at the Anglo-Chinese Junior College in Shanghai. There, he was briefly exposed to English, Western sciences and geography, before a bout of typhoid fever led to his early removal from the school. But it was while at the College that Koo experienced one of the defining incidents in his life and ideology. Deciding to try out his new bicycle near the Shanghai racecourse one Saturday, he found himself riding behind another cyclist, a British boy from the International Settlement. At some point, the British boy rode up onto the sidewalk, and the young Koo followed him. The boy cycled past an Indian policeman, who ignored him, but who immediately stopped Koo.

Ignoring all protests, the policeman handed Koo over to the Chinese authorities, who took him to the local police station, impounded his bicycle, and refused to release it until he paid a fine of five *yuan* for cycling on the pavement.

I don't know the rule, protested the 11-year-old Koo. *I only followed that English boy.*[5]

It was an object lesson in extraterritoriality. A foreign boy had been permitted to break a law with impunity, while a Chinese native, who had not even known that an infraction had taken place, had been arrested by a foreign police officer. The damage to Koo's finances was minimal – he immediately stomped back to his sister's house to pick up the money – but the incident was to forever shape his attitude towards international diplomacy.

2
The Open Door

Opposition to foreigners found new inspirations and new outlets in the Shandong region, where the arrival of German and British occupiers soon put Europeans at odds with the locals. At one village, missionaries occupied a building they claimed to have been a long-abandoned church, dating back to the 17th century, whereas locals could not remember a time when it had not been used simply as a temple. The missionaries in the area rode roughshod over long-established traditions and beliefs – local interests, who took particular exception to the missionaries' status, regarded the sharp spires and crosses of their buildings as bad *feng shui*. The Emperor had conferred high authority on the new arrivals, and their own special laws left them exempt from Chinese justice.

The Society of the Righteous and Harmonious Fist, better known as the Boxers, began in the midst of such complaints. Their initial aims, like many less successful secret societies, was the expulsion of all foreigners, which included the overthrow of the ruling Qing dynasty, who were the descendants of 17th century invaders from Manchuria. Over time, however, imperial agents persuaded the Boxers to refocus their activities as a loyalist movement, still dedicated to expelling foreigners from China, but doing so in the name of the Emperor they had once planned to oust.

The Boxers were a traditionalist sect, and gained their nickname from European observers who saw their martial arts training. It was believed by the Boxers that the refinement of their spirit through martial arts would render them invulnerable to foreign bullets and make them invincible in battle. With echoes of the Taiping cult of the previous generation, some also believed that angelic 'spirit soldiers' would descend from heaven to help them deal with the foreign invaders.

In January 1900, the imperial government even issued tentative proclamations in support of the Boxers' aims. By June the same year, a Boxer army, tellingly augmented with supporters from the imperial army, descended on Beijing, killing over 200 foreigners. The foreigners in Beijing retreated to their Legation Quarter, an area of several city blocks in central Beijing, which was fortified for a siege that eventually lasted 55 days.

The Empress Dowager, who held imperial authority in the name of her nephew the Emperor, then proclaimed war against all foreigners in China. It was a sign of her declining power that few in the provinces dared to follow her command, but in Beijing the foreigners were left to fight for their lives. The siege of the Foreign Legations became an international *cause célèbre*, and was lifted by the arrival of a multi-national military force in July. As a result of the Boxer Rebellion, the Chinese government was fined 450 million taels in war reparations, payable over a 39-year period, during which time interest accrued would take the total up to almost a billion.

To collect the money, the foreign powers gained further

control of China's trade tariffs and salt tax, which were increased in order to generate the necessary income.

With foreign armies exchanging fire with rebels only a block away from the Emperor's official residence in Beijing, the Boxer Rebellion was a mortal blow to the ruling Qing dynasty. It helped revive the belief among many Chinese that the Emperor himself was an unwelcome foreign invader, and that China's fortunes could only improve if the Qing dynasty were overthrown. For other Chinese, however, including the Gu family, the foreign incursions gained a more positive spin. The foreigners were, after all, victorious. If one believed their appeal to free trade, and reparations,

> A tael is an ounce of silver. Hence, in 2008 currency, 450 million taels approximate to £4 billion (US$8 billion).

and justice, then one might also believe that the foreigners knew something that the Chinese did not. If China was in the wrong, ignorant of some nebulous international code of conduct, then surely it was in China's best interests to learn from the invaders, in order to avoid making the same mistakes in the future? This was certainly the attitude that was fostered in the young Wellington Koo by his schoolmasters. China was wrong, the West was right, and the only way for China to drag itself out of its shame was to learn from the foreigners.

Koo did not return to the Anglo-Chinese Junior College, but enrolled for 1900–1 in the Talent Fostering School, also in Shanghai.[1] In 1903, Koo studied at St John's College, an American missionary school. The tutors at St John's were determined to beat outdated ideas and attitudes out of the Chinese, and decried the 'false history, false science, false geography, false chronology, false philosophy ... [and] false religion' of Chinese traditional education. *Apparently*, Koo commented, *the aim of a missionary school was to train*

Chinese not with a view to what China needed as a nation, but what the missionary movement needed.[2]

Despite compulsory prayer meetings, Bible studies and mandatory church attendance, St John's did not turn Koo into a Christian. Instead, he remembered his college as a place of cold rooms, harsh discipline and bad food. The middle Koo brother also attended, but fell victim to the system when he was expelled for reading an English book in Chinese class. This left Wellington as the sole family beneficiary from the St John's curriculum – Eurocentric language, literature and history, all taught in English. The school was resolutely, some might say bloody-mindedly Anglophone, and it turned the young Koo into a fluent English-speaker before he was out of his teens – he even reputedly edited its English year book, *Dragon Flag*.[3] It also put him in touch with an 'old boy' network that included many influential figures of the 20th century, including Alfred Sze and T V Soong.

Late in Koo's schooldays, a change in policy by the board of governors placed the study of Chinese language and history on an equal footing with that of English. Several Chinese lecturers were appointed who had studied abroad in the progressive nation of Japan, but few of them lasted long – their notions of Asian-centred independence and thought were found to be unsettlingly radical by the American missionaries.

Many students of Koo's generation studied in Japan, but St John's offered him a unique opportunity. Alumni connections gave him the chance to study at the alma mater of some of his American teachers. In 1903, he left for America, in the company of St John's alumnus Alfred Sze, who was leading a group of students on government scholarships.

Wellington Koo was only 15 years old when he finished his studies at St John's. His parents waved him off from Shanghai with pride, his father saying to his mother: 'We need never worry about this son.'[4]

Koo lived frugally in the United States, staying at a rooming house where he developed a lifelong love of American breakfasts, particularly hash-brown potatoes, about which his family would tease him for decades. Between 1904 and 1905, when Japan went on to shock the world by fighting another war in Korea and Manchuria, this time against Russia, Koo was studying in Ithaca at the Cook Academy. His father's decision to send him to St John's was validated in 1905, when the Qing government abolished the imperial examination system. Old knowledge, of the Confucian variety, was no longer regarded to be of use in the acquisition of government positions – future political careers in the Chinese government would go to people like Koo, and his fellow graduates of the many progressive, 'modern' schools set up in the wake of the abolition.

Modernists like the young Koo undertook their studies in the expectation that China's lowly position in world affairs could be averted by joining the international community. However, they were also aware that China did not yet deal with the foreign powers on equal terms. Even as some foreign powers spoke of the need to respect each other's territorial integrity, they enjoyed special privileges in China that were not granted elsewhere.

The Open Door principle had been implicit in many of the former treaties concluded between China and foreign powers. It formed part of the demands for Most Favoured Nation status, which a practical diplomat might read as a demand for all countries to enjoy equal trade rights with each other. For this to be enforceable, those same countries would need to agree not to enforce preferential duties or conditions for themselves, and that in turn would require all countries to respect the legal and territorial integrity of any other country in which they operated.

John Hay, the United States Secretary of State from 1898 to 1905, circulated a memorandum that called for other powers to respect China's territorial integrity. He was concerned, initially, about Russian encroachment into Manchuria, which was itself halted and replaced by Japanese encroachment in the wake of the Russo-Japanese War in 1905.

The policy, to which foreign powers eventually agreed with some reluctance, would influence the next 30 years of international politics in China. In particular, it would be a perpetual issue between the US and Japan, the first manifestation of which was the bilateral Root-Takahira Agreement of 1908. This deal allowed for Japan to recognise the American occupation of Hawaii and the Philippines, and to agree to limits on Japanese immigration to California. In return, the US agreed to recognise Japan's annexation of Korea, and its 'interests' in Manchuria.

One result of the Open Door policy was the establishment of an international banking consortium to provide loans to China for railway construction. In theory, this would stop any single country from claiming ownership and hence influence on a railway. It was hoped that this would prevent recurrences of conflicts such as that between Russia and Japan over railway rights in Manchuria that had led to the Russo-Japanese War.

Despite the fact that all signatories of the Open Door policy ignored its tenets at one time or another, it did at least theoretically establish China's right to self-determination. It would lead Chinese intellectuals to assume that if China could supply a modern administration and a democratic society, a competent police force and a law-abiding society, that the injustices of the Unequal Treaties could be gradually lifted, until China was a fully participatory member of the international community. It was with such an aim in mind that young scholars like Wellington Koo chose to study abroad.

While they were away, imperial China continued to take steps towards modernisation. In 1906, the government promised to draft a constitution. In 1909, there were steps towards the setting-up of provincial assemblies, and even a move in 1910 to form a parliament. Political reform, however, was often thwarted. Conservative factions within the government often ruined genuine attempts at reform, by bogging them down with stipulations – the insistence, for example, that a supposedly democratic assembly be largely composed of Manchu princes. Meanwhile, hardliners often watched for radical activity and then persecuted the radicals, so that even as the government promised reform, many would-be reformers were imprisoned or executed.

From 1905 to 1908 Wellington Koo studied liberal arts at Columbia University, where he threw himself into conspicuous college activities; he was elected to several student societies, won the Columbia-Cornell debating medal, was editor-in-chief of the *Columbia Daily Spectator* and was on the track team.[5]

By 1908, Koo, now 20 years old, had become the president of the Chinese Students' Association in America, a grand union of many student societies at other US universities. In this capacity, he was invited to Washington along with 40 other student leaders to meet an illustrious Chinese visitor. Tang Shaoyi (1859–1938) had been sent as an ambassador of the Qing dynasty, but was also on the lookout for successful students for employment back in China.

SUN YATSEN'S THREE PRINCIPLES

Much of the rhetoric of Chinese reform came not from China itself, but from overseas Chinese communities, scattered in Chinatowns around the world. The most vocal overseas Chinese reformer was Sun Yatsen (1866–1925). Sun was from southern China, but had been educated in American-occupied Hawaii, and technically was an American citizen. Sun was the leader of a coalition of several political groups whose broad aim was the establishment of democracy in China. Sun was an ideal poster-boy for the revolution abroad; he had learned English in Hawaii, was a baptised Christian, and had a Hong Kong medical degree. He was particularly popular in Japan, where in 1905 he formulated his Three Principles of the People: *Minzu, Minquan, Minsheng*, which might be roughly translated, with a nod to the Gettysburg Address that may have inspired them, as 'Government of the people, by the people, for the people'.

In a Chinese context, this meant, *Minzu* – representation of all the peoples in China, not merely the ruling Manchu minority, but with an equal voice for the dominant Han ethnic group, and, it was implied, ethnic minorities such as Chinese Muslims, Tibetans, Hakka and other races. A radical idea at the time, Sun's principle called for China to be a national concept, and for the various races China contained to identify as Chinese, not as competing rival groups who happened to live on Chinese territory. *Minquan* – the second principle took this idea further, demanding that the groups thus represented would be governed by democratically elected representatives in a constitutional assembly. *Minsheng* – livelihood, the recognition of key areas such as food, clothing, housing and transportation, necessary for the welfare of all. The third principle hence set down certain aims and duties for this theoretical government. In total, Sun Yatsen's Three Principles were a powerful blueprint for turning China into a modern state, and precisely the sort of reform that Western allies might hope for.

Koo returned home to Shanghai for the summer vacation, where he was obliged to fulfil the promise his father made to Doctor Zhang. He married Zhang's daughter, a sheltered, traditional Chinese girl, who returned to America with him as he commenced his postgraduate studies. Far away from home in an alien culture, the new Mrs Koo did not last long, and soon fled home, from where she would eventually sue for divorce.

Alone in America once more, Koo studied for a Master's, and then a Ph.D in political science at Columbia. His chief tutor was John Bassett Moore, a specialist in international law and the author of *Reports on Extraterritorial Crime* (1887). It is no surprise that with such an influence and his own experiences, Koo would chose to focus on extraterritoriality himself. He confided to his diary that the idea had been pushed by Moore's research assistant, Winifred Scott, as a valuable component in securing a diplomatic career. *It would*, he wrote, *put me in the best position to deal with China's foreign relations later – to see how China was mistreated, denied the rights to which a sovereign nation was entitled under international law.*[6]

His interest was not merely in the abuses of extraterritoriality in China, but in the inherent hypocrisy – many foreign powers argued for the inalienable rights of man, but refused to offer the same rights to the Chinese in their own country. In his Ph.D dissertation, *The Status of Aliens in China*, Koo wrote: *The ... complex problems which arise out of [foreigners'] intercourse with the Chinese people depend for their prompt solution primarily upon an accurate knowledge of the rights, privileges and immunities which they are*

John Bassett Moore (1860–1947) had held Columbia's first professorship in international law since its creation in 1891. He was often seconded to government posts, including secretarial posts at conferences on colonial matters, and taught briefly at the American Naval College, where he initiated the 'Blue Books' in international law. In later life, his career would foreshadow that of his Chinese pupil: he was a strong proponent of American neutrality, and warned that the post-First World War settlement would lead to another global conflict. He served on the Hague Tribunal (1912–38) and the International Court (1921–8).

entitled to enjoy under laws and treaties, and of the limitations ... arising ... .[7]

While Koo was working on his dissertation, China underwent a radical change in its government. The imperial institution, which supposedly dated back to the dawn of time, was brought to a crushing halt. In 1908, the Emperor had died, suspiciously close to the date of death of the Empress Dowager herself, leading many to suspect that one or both had been poisoned. The new Son of Heaven was a squalling infant, Puyi, whose father's attempts to mollify him during his coronation with the words 'Don't cry, soon this will all be over' were later regarded as a prophecy of disaster. Floods and droughts soon led to food shortages in the countryside, where the locals were already paying heavier taxes to help pay foreign indemnities and fund the modernisation of distant urban locations.

Railways, those vital but expensive conduits of trade, helped push China further towards revolution. Worried about stalling railway construction, the imperial government had nationalised a critical line in the southern provinces before seeking a foreign loan to fund further developments. This decision was met with strong protests from many southerners, whose own investments were now null and void, ironically cancelled by their own government in the quest to put China deeper in debt to foreigners. Demonstrations soon turned into a full-scale uprising, with the protestors occupying the city of Wuchang, capital of Hubei province. Chinese soldiers soon joined in the uprising – ironically many of the rebels were working to paradigms set and stirred up by revolutionary propaganda from the likes of Sun Yatsen, although Sun was out of the country at the time.

Desperate to control the new rebellion, the imperial

government called in Yuan Shikai (1859–1916), the commander of the Beiyang Army. Far from saving his imperial
masters, Yuan instead opened negotiations on both sides.
Yuan hoped to move reforms forward even faster by securing
the resignation of the Emperor, whose last act would be to
appoint him as head of state. But even as Yuan prepared to
become the first president of the newly proclaimed Republic
of China, he discovered that someone had got there ahead of
him. Far to the south in Nanjing, Sun Yatsen had arrived in
China, where the exiled revolutionary thinker was acclaimed
as the ideal candidate to lead China into its early days as a
republic.

The messy Chinese revolution had secured the abdication
of the Last Emperor, who would continue to dwell in retirement in his vast palace complex in central Beijing. However,
it inadvertently created two rival governments, who would
struggle over the right to rule China for the ensuing 15 years.
Sun Yatsen was nominally China's first president, although his
tenure lasted barely long enough for him to resign in favour
of Yuan Shikai, whose access to the Beiyang Army gave him
an unanswerable authority.

Koo's dissertation was still lacking a final chapter when
he received a telegram from Tang Shaoyi, now back in China
and the Premier of the new Chinese Republic. Recalling the
talents of the young man he had first met in Washington in
1908, Tang offered him a job as the English-language secretary to the Republican President. After consulting with John
Bassett Moore, Koo returned to China by the long route, via
Europe and the Trans-Siberian Railway. During his journey,
his dissertation was edited and published by the faculty of
political science at Columbia.

Koo's new boss was a controversial figure, remembered by

history as a warlord and despot who would eventually try to have himself proclaimed a new Emperor. Having twice failed in the imperial civil service examinations, Yuan instead chose a military career. In the 1880s, he was the leader of Chinese expeditionary forces in Korea, and became 'Imperial Resident' in Seoul. He was governor of Shandong at the turn of the century, and came to foreign attention when he helped in the suppression of the Boxer Rebellion. Enjoying the support of the Beiyang Army, even when out of favour in Beijing, he finally accepted the post of Prime Minister in late 1911. With the fall of the Last Emperor, Yuan Shikai was faced with the news that the revolutionary southern government had elected Sun Yatsen as the new president of the Republic of China. However, Yuan Shikai was able to engineer Sun's swift resignation in his own favour – Sun lacked an army, and it was still unclear at the time if the imperial institution had entirely fallen, or was simply about to be replaced with a constitutional monarchy. Yuan Shikai's deal with the Republicans called for him to finalise the abdication of the Last Emperor (a six-year-old boy) in the early weeks of 1912. In return, Yuan was made the new President of the Republic.

Koo was hired both as Yuan's English-language secretary and one of eight secretaries to Yuan's provisional cabinet. However, Yuan had risen to power as a military man, and gave democracy little thought. Tang Shaoyi soon fell out with Yuan over Yuan's attitude towards the political process; when Tang resigned and went south, Koo followed him as far as Tianjin before being tempted back with a second secretarial position, as assistant to the Foreign Minister, W W Yen. This new appointment was the commencement of his diplomatic career – it kept him close to the government, but largely aloof from domestic struggles.

Domestic connections of a more personal nature also sealed Koo's position within the new China. By 1913, the stalemate with the first Mrs Koo had been laid to rest, and Koo was granted a divorce. He had complained, with a certain sense of modernity, that the Chinese tradition for arranged marriages such as his, in which the bride and groom did not even meet until the day of their wedding, was responsible for uncountable numbers of unhappy couples. But in June of the same year, Koo wed his second wife in an arrangement that, although it contained a façade of happenstance and romance, was no less 'arranged' than his first marriage.

The second Mrs Koo was a girl whom Wellington had first met when her father had asked him to chaperone her and her sisters on a trip to the Temple of Heaven in Beijing. Her name was Tang Baoyu, although she usually went by her 'English' name of May. More notably for a man on Koo's career path, she was the daughter of Tang Shaoyi, the recently-resigned Prime Minister, whose disagreement with Yuan Shikai had led him to seek new allies in the southern government of Sun Yatsen. Koo, thus enjoyed connections of some sort with both major areas of political influence in modern China.

Chinese politics remained tense, often on the brink of civil war. Like Tang Shaoyi, the revolutionary south soon lost patience with Yuan Shikai, regarding him as just one more warlord. A democratic opposition foundered with the suspicious death of its leading candidate, and Yuan's bluff, rough-shod attitude towards his government often drew criticism. Meanwhile, at the edges of what had once been the Chinese empire, independence movements went unanswered – Mongolia and Tibet both proclaimed independence in 1911.

And yet, while admitting that Yuan was authoritarian, Koo remained staunchly supportive of the dictator, noting that he was *painstaking in his handling of foreign relations and made himself responsible for what the government did.*[8] In later life, Koo would praise Yuan as a great leader, an able administrator and a patriot – a controversial opinion greatly at odds with that of most historians.

Despite the allegations of corruption, Yuan remained aware of and engaged with the threat posed to China by the outside world. The United States, in the form of its president Woodrow Wilson, unilaterally recognised Yuan's government as the legitimate authority in China in 1913, and other nations soon followed suit.

3
The Twenty-One Demands

The outbreak of the First World War split the northern Chinese government over the best means of action. China's first act, on 6 August 1914, was to claim Chinese territory and Chinese waters to be off-limits to 'belligerent operations' – a statement borne out of the very real fear that, like Korea before it, sovereign Chinese terrain might become a battleground between two foreign powers. However, the Chinese were too late – determined to free up forces for the war in Europe, the British called upon the provisions of their Japanese Alliance. In the interests of protecting British shipping elsewhere, the Japanese were expected to neutralise the German naval presence in Asia; this, inevitably, would entail an attack on Shandong.

Japan opened hostilities in the same month, with a communiqué to the Germans, demanding the surrender of their naval base at Qingdao. Koo, who had already worked on the draft proclamation of Chinese neutrality, was sent to the American embassy in Beijing in the hope of heading the deal off. He made the far-fetched suggestion that America could persuade Britain and Germany to mutually agree that

Shandong could be handed back to China, and thereby avoid any hostilities there.

Divisions within Yuan Shikai's government were split between a 'reserved faction', that hoped to preserve Chinese neutrality, and a 'realistic faction' which argued that China's best chance of not suffering from the war was to enter it on the winning side. Although Koo had faithfully served the 'reserved' interests in his diplomatic meetings in 1914, he personally favoured the 'realist' argument, and advised Yuan Shikai of this in a cabinet meeting.

Determined to stay neutral, Yuan sent Koo to try another tactic. Koo brought up the Root-Takahira Agreement of 1908 with the Americans, particularly the clause in which Japan and the United States agreed to respect China's territorial integrity. Surely, he argued, this must mean that Japan was obliged to consult the US before landing troops in China – the ideal opportunity for America to warn the Japanese off? However, America was understandably reluctant to place itself on a war footing against two putative allies merely to defend a territory that was not even under Chinese control, and Washington quickly found a loophole. The powers were only expected to consult each other 'in the case of internal disorders in China', and a Japanese invasion of Shandong was not 'internal'.

In a futile gesture, the 'reserved' faction in Beijing imposed a war zone around Qingdao on 3 December, hoping to discourage the Japanese from crossing an imaginary line. The Japanese ignored this entirely, landing troops on the peninsula on the same day. The Germans soon surrendered, effectively handing Shandong over to Japanese control.

Koo made repeated efforts to solicit American intercession over the incident, calling on the American Minister in Beijing,

Paul Reinsch. Reinsch commiserated with the earnest, well-spoken, American-educated young diplomat, and sent several cables of his own to Washington, lamenting America's unwillingness to help a state that hoped to emulate it. Koo also made sure that the press was kept well informed about Japanese injustices, in the hope that world opinion could be turned against the Japanese.

On 18 January 1915, Japan presented China with a series of Twenty-One Demands, drafted by the incumbent Japanese prime minister Ōkuma Shigenobu, approved by his cabinet, and printed, in a superfluous and rather ominous flourish, on paper that bore a watermark of dreadnoughts and machine guns.[1] The demands were a blatant move to bully China into handing over territory ahead of the end of hostilities; many of the demands only made sense if one assumed, as the Japanese did, that the war and subsequent Peace Conference would see the Western Powers losing influence in Asia, and creating a new vacuum of influence and conquest that the Japanese hoped to fill. They were summarised in five groups:

Paul Samuel Reinsch (1869–1923), born in Milwaukee, was the son of German immigrants. Graduating in law from the university of Wisconsin-Madison in 1892, he practised as a lawyer before becoming a professor of political science. He became America's Minister in China in 1913, where he grew increasingly disillusioned with his government's policy towards the Chinese. He eventually resigned, warning that Japan's activities in the Far East would one day escalate into a world war.

1. The Japanese acquisition of Shandong was confirmed (i.e. left to Japan, the *de facto* occupier, and Germany, the soon-to-be-vanquished former occupier, to determine).
2. Japan was to gain further rights of settlement and

occupation along the South Manchuria Railway, effectively extending Japanese influence into Manchuria itself.

3. Several Chinese mines and refineries with Japanese shareholders were to be handed over to full Japanese control.
4. China was to offer no further territorial concessions to foreign powers, except Japan.
5. A cluster of further deals establishing Japanese control of the Chinese police force, Chinese arms trade, Chinese government offices, and the vague yet intimidating right of Japanese missionaries to 'preach' in China.

The Twenty-One Demands came attached to honeyed rationalisations, that it was for China's own good, and that by 'demanding' them by force, Japan was allowing the Chinese government to save face with its own people and with the international community, as inviting Japan to do the same would have been embarrassing.[2] They also contained veiled threats, that if Yuan did not agree, Japan would instead find a group of Chinese revolutionaries who would, and would then offer sufficient support to the revolutionaries in order to topple Yuan's government. It was the diplomacy of the bully, urging China to act as if already defeated, in order to avoid an actual, physical invasion. It was also intensely secretive – Japan wanted the agreement to be made without the knowledge of the international community. Behind the scenes, Koo blew his top, not merely at the Japanese harassment, but at Lu Zhengxiang's intention to ask the Japanese to approve China's reply before it was filed. When informed of this by the Australian foreign adviser William Donald, Koo reportedly 'exploded like a string of Chinese firecrackers'.

They send you an ultimatum and you ask them please to

draw up your reply? he said. *You people call yourselves dip-lomats! Why you are nothing but stupid fools! This is why we are eating Japanese dirt – because China has too many people who cannot see beyond their rice bowls. They live for today, not for the tomorrows. They are children with no perspective. They do not stand upon their two feet and say that they are men, nor when they fail, do they have bad dreams. There is always the opium house, the singsong girl, the feasts, or the retreat to the mountain to live in seclusion amid the luxury of ill-gotten gains.*[3]

Yuan Shikai was unsurprised that the Japanese had tried such a bold move while the other imperial powers were preoc-cupied with a war in Europe. Perhaps aware of his previous press leaks, the Japanese refused to permit Koo's presence at the secret negotiations that followed. Koo, however, played his part by getting as much information about the Twenty-One Demands as was possible to foreign contacts.

> They send you an ultimatum and you ask them please to draw up your reply? You people call yourselves diplomats! Why you are nothing but stupid fools!
>
> **WELLINGTON KOO**

Initially, his leaks were mistaken for scaremongering, with neither the Americans nor British believing the claims, particularly those in the fifth group. Eventually, Wilson was persuaded, and publicly stated on 13 March that America would continue to support the Open Door policy. Britain made similar noises, but neither power would actively inter-fere, since both hoped to preserve their relationship with Japan. Ironically, when America took a stronger position against Japan, one Japanese baron was heard to complain that the United States had become entirely inept at dealing with foreign affairs since John Bassett Moore had ceased working for the Department of State. In fact, Wilson was being persuaded by one of Moore's greatest pupils, Wellington Koo.[4]

Japanese bluster was not only being brought to bear on the Chinese. The Australian Billy Hughes, later to be such a thorn in the Japanese delegates' side at Versailles, discovered that the Japanese had been twisting the British arm as well. 'When I saw Lord Grey,' wrote Hughes, 'and complained that Australia had not been consulted – or even notified – of Japan's annexation [of the Carolines, Marshals and Marianas], he told me that a few weeks previously the Japanese Ambassador had personally notified him that unless Japan's annexation was recognized by Britain, she would forthwith ally herself with Germany.'[5]

Koo's efforts behind the scenes achieved something – Japan offered to drop the fifth group of demands, but still insisted that China accept the others by 9 May. Failure to do so would result in a declaration of war. Yuan made the Japanese wait an extra couple of weeks, but caved in on 25 May. His generals advised war, but Yuan doubted that the Chinese military was in any position to resist. Koo himself, now convalescing in a hospital bed from an unspecified illness, drafted the Chinese response to the Japanese. In doing so, Koo deliberately couched the language of the Chinese agreement in terms that he hoped would be renegotiable at a later stage. Since everyone expected that the war would be followed by a Peace Conference at which various treaties could be discussed, Koo was careful to note in his draft that China had been 'constrained to comply with the full terms of the Ultimatum'. Years later in Paris, Koo would cling to his own wording as evidence that China had been forced into its deal with Japan, and that Japan consequently did not have a leg to stand on. Koo's wording also carefully restated a Chinese interest in 'equal opportunity' for all nations in China. By this, Koo hoped to use the Unequal Treaties to China's advantage, encouraging other powers to regard the Japanese incursion on Chinese territory as an assault on *their* interests – this rhetorical appeal would be something he would continue to employ throughout his diplomatic career. Before the Paris Peace Conference had even been scheduled, it had become China's last hope of extricating itself from the deals made in 1915, and one on which Koo was already banking.[6]

Yuan and his advisers were sure the Japanese would soon be back to try another approach. The events set his mind on a muddled policy of restoring China to the status of a monarchy, all the better to deal with Japan in a 'meeting of minds'. It is unclear how Yuan thought this might help, although there were sure to be new issues of protocol, as the Japanese emperor had been officially a vassal of the Chinese emperor, at least on paper, for centuries. Yuan nevertheless appears to have believed that returning China to some form of monarchy, at first through a military dictatorship, was the best way to resist Japan, and sent Wellington Koo to Washington to smooth the decision over with the Americans.

Koo was sent first to Mexico, but this was merely a means of putting him on the promotional ladder. It seems he was always intended to be the Chinese minister in Washington, but for the sake of propriety his bosses gave the young man an official 'minor' post first. Koo was still *en route* to take it up when he was informed that he had been promoted to be China's minister in the United States in October 1915

– the promotion of a existing minister looked better on paper than the truth, which was that Koo had no diplomatic experience.

He arrived with a substantial salary and an even larger monthly entertainment allowance, with which he was expected to wine and dine American officials into accepting that China was not yet ready for an American-style democratic republic. Even as he began his mission, Koo observed to one American that he doubted his chances. While Koo was away, Yuan organised a congress that 'voted' unanimously to restore the imperial institution, with Yuan as the new Emperor of Constitutional Abundance. He met, however, with a remarkable degree of resistance – Lu Zhengxiang, for example, pointedly refused the offer of the rank of Marquis in the new aristocracy.[7] Yuan soon lost many of the prized advisers he had hoped to buy with noble ranks, and the move met with resistance all over China (backed in part, of course, by the Japanese), and as provincial governors began to proclaim their objection and *de facto* rebellion, Yuan's support melted away. Yuan's enthronement ceremony was repeatedly postponed, its budget cut and then eventually cancelled, and the 57-year-old Yuan, already ill with kidney problems, died in June 1916. His last act, an attempt to unify China, had only unified it in opposition to himself – with him gone, many of his leading opponents were now leaders of their own armies, and prepared to fight for control over parcels of China. Yuan's death ushered in the 'warlord era' of 20th-century China. Far removed from the unrest in his home country, Koo was now a representative of an unknown regime.

By October 1916, Beijing was under the control of a new warlord, Duan Qirui, whose mastery of the capital made him

Koo's new boss. There was also a new regime in Japan, where a change in government had led to a brief thaw in Sino-Japanese relations. Koo advised Duan against dealing with the Japanese, but Duan favoured loans from Japanese banks over those on offer from other powers, dragging China further into the Japanese sphere of influence.

Koo suspected, rightly, that the Allies had already agreed, in secret and without consulting the Chinese, that the Japanese could keep Qingdao in exchange for wartime cooperation. He reasoned that America was the only country that did not have a 'dark scheme' for China – every other Power had or seemed to want concessions, and Koo counselled Beijing that China's best chance of securing a fair deal once the war was over would come from ensuring that it was clearly on the winning side. Before China even entered the war, Koo could see that Japan would seek to benefit from its position as one of the Allies – China needed to be too, or its voice would not be heard.[8]

Trained as an artilleryman at the Tianjin military academy, Duan Qirui (1864–1936) was sent by Li Hongzhang to study in Germany. He subsequently became an instructor at the Weihai military academy, and became a leading figure in Yuan Shikai's army. He alternated as Prime Minister and Minister of War in several governments between 1912 and 1918, and would become provisional President in 1924.

Eventually, it was Germany itself that provoked China into entering the war, or at least provided a valid enough excuse. On 24 February 1917, the French ship *Athos* was sunk by a German submarine – the Kaiser having authorised a resumption of unrestricted submarine warfare. The *Athos* sank with the loss of 543 Chinese lives, as it had been carrying coolies to help with the war effort. A Chinese protest to Germany was rejected on 10 March, but still the incumbent President Li

Yuan-hong refused to break neutrality. An angry Duan Qirui went through the motions of resigning in protest, but was soon reinstated with his request granted – China severed diplomatic relations with Germany on 14 March.[9]

The return to unrestricted submarine warfare was also a significant influence on Woodrow Wilson. Although he had secured re-election on a campaign promise to keep America out of the war in Europe, he was persuaded to change his mind by the resumption of U-Boat attacks, combined with the unearthing by British intelligence of a secret communiqué, the 'Zimmermann Telegram' that encouraged Mexico and Japan to ally with each other and attack America. Congress voted to declare war on 6 April 1917, after Wilson had given a speech alluding to his interests in fighting for 'the rights and liberties of small nations'. Behind the scenes, the back-door communications between China and the US established that China would follow Wilson in declaring war. However, it would be fairer to say that Beijing declared war – the rival Chinese government in the south was aghast at the news, and remained critical of it.

Koo got what he wanted on 14 August, when China officially declared war on Germany. However, this only created new problems elsewhere. In Canton, Sun Yatsen suddenly gained enough funding to set up a rival government, under the auspices of the Movement to Protect the Constitution. Although it had the rhetoric of pacifism and diplomacy, its seed money was believed to have been supplied by the German consulate in Shanghai, which was hoping to cut down China's war effort by destabilising the Beijing administration that had proclaimed it.[10]

Even among China's allies, there were secret deals that would have an adverse affect on China. On 2 November 1917, the United States and Japan concluded the Lansing-Ishii Agreement, in which both countries pledged to uphold the Open Door policy on China. America, in return, recognised that Japan had special interests in Manchuria, and a secret codicil, which would soon turn out to be not worth the paper it was printed on, included a further agreement that neither would use the war to gain unilateral advantage in China. America, it seems, interpreted this as an agreement by Japan not to keep hold of Shandong. Japan, conversely, seems to have interpreted this as an agreement that Japan could continue to do whatever it liked, as long as other Powers acted in a similar fashion.

A second American project was more likely to offer hope to Koo. A committee of inquiry, headed by Colonel Edward House, had delivered a report to Woodrow Wilson outlining the topics likely to arise at a putative post-war Peace Conference, and the ideological position that would best serve Wilson's proposed League of Nations. In anticipation of these issues, on 8 January 1918, Wilson delivered a speech to the US Congress outlining his Fourteen Points, including open covenants on peace, free trade, and the right of nations to self-determination. Wilson's points made several direct references to issues of the day, such as the presence of foreign troops in Russia, the need for a Polish state, and the future fate of Turkish territory. There was, however, no direct reference to China or Japan, and Wilson's Points were chiefly European in their outlook and aims.

Wilson's speech was intended to set the agenda for a peace conference after a German defeat that many now regarded as inevitable. The Fourteen Points were also intended as a propaganda strike against Germany, a pre-emptive offer of terms for an armistice, outlining what America regarded as

PRESIDENT WILSON'S FOURTEEN POINTS, 8 JANUARY 1918

The program of the world's peace, therefore, is our program; and that program, the only possible program, as we see it, is this:

I. Open covenants of peace, openly arrived at, after which there shall be no private international understandings of any kind but diplomacy shall proceed always frankly and in the public view.

II. Absolute freedom of navigation upon the seas, outside territorial waters, alike in peace and in war, except as the seas may be closed in whole or in part by international action for the enforcement of international covenants.

III. The removal, so far as possible, of all economic barriers and the establishment of an equality of trade conditions among all the nations consenting to the peace and associating themselves for its maintenance.

IV. Adequate guarantees given and taken that national armaments will be reduced to the lowest point consistent with domestic safety.

V. A free, open-minded, and absolutely impartial adjustment of all colonial claims, based upon a strict observance of the principle that in determining all such questions of sovereignty the interests of the populations concerned must have equal weight with the equitable claims of the government whose title is to be determined.

VI. The evacuation of all Russian territory and such a settlement of all questions affecting Russia as will secure the best and freest cooperation of the other nations of the world in obtaining for her an unhampered and unembarrassed opportunity for the independent determination of her own political development and national policy and assure her of a sincere welcome into the society of free nations under institutions of her own choosing; and, more than a welcome, assistance also of every kind that she may need and may herself desire. The treatment accorded Russia by her sister nations in the months to come will be the acid test of their good will, of their comprehension of her needs as distinguished from their own interests, and of their intelligent and unselfish sympathy.

VII. Belgium, the whole world will agree, must be evacuated and restored, without any attempt to limit the sovereignty which she enjoys in common with all other free nations. No other single act will serve as this will serve to restore confidence among the nations in the laws which they have themselves set and determined for the government of their relations with one another. Without this healing act the whole structure and validity of international law is forever impaired.

VIII. All French territory should be freed and the invaded portions restored, and the wrong done to France by Prussia in 1871 in the matter of Alsace-Lorraine, which has unsettled the peace of the world for nearly fifty years, should be righted, in order that peace may once more be made secure in the interest of all.

IX. A readjustment of the frontiers of Italy should be effected along clearly recognizable lines of nationality.

X. The peoples of Austria-Hungary, whose place among the nations we wish to see safeguarded and assured, should be accorded the freest opportunity to autonomous development.

XI. Rumania, Serbia, and Montenegro should be evacuated; occupied territories restored; Serbia accorded free and secure access to the sea; and the relations of the several Balkan states to one another determined by friendly counsel along historically established lines of allegiance and nationality; and international guarantees of the political and economic independence and territorial integrity of the several Balkan states should be entered into.

XII. The Turkish portion of the present Ottoman Empire should be assured a secure sovereignty, but the other nationalities which are now under Turkish rule should be assured an undoubted security of life and an absolutely unmolested opportunity of autonomous development, and the Dardanelles should be permanently opened as a free passage to the ships and commerce of all nations under international guarantees.

XIII. An independent Polish state should be erected which should include the territories inhabited by indisputably Polish populations, which should be assured a free and secure access to the sea, and whose political and economic independence and territorial integrity should be guaranteed by international covenant.

XIV. A general association of nations must be formed under specific covenants for the purpose of affording mutual guarantees of political independence and territorial integrity to great and small states alike.

reasonable terms. In this, they were influential to a degree, although since Wilson had made his speech without soliciting the opinion of his European allies, they also opened new debates on issues that divided them. Ten months later, when Germany finally sought an armistice, the Fourteen Points would form the basic agenda for the discussion of peace, and for the Peace Conference that was convened in Paris.

In a meeting with his advisers in October 1918 to discuss China's role at the Peace Conference, Duan Qirui offered a surprisingly measured outline of reasonable aims: 'China joined the allies at a very late date and only in name, therefore our claims should be accordingly confined to a few items, such as restoration of German and Austrian concessions, abrogation of Articles ... permitting signatory powers to keep permanent guards for their legations, and to station troops between the capital and the sea; and the restoration of tariff autonomy. As for the [Shandong] problem, Japan has repeatedly declared that she would agree to the reversion to China of the interests she has taken over from Germany ... . It is fairly certain that she will not break the promise.' [11]

Duan's conciliatory tone, and his rather naïve faith in the Japanese, hid a dark secret. Unknown to many lesser officials, including Koo, who was still in Washington, Duan had already made a series of concessions to the Japanese in return for important bank loans. On 28 September 1918, with the end of the war imminent, Duan concluded a deal with Japan in which the Chinese government 'gladly agreed' to allow Japan to station troops along a strategically important Shandong railway. In return, Japanese cash would prop up Duan's regime. Duan's deal with the Japanese would hobble much of Koo's efforts to unravel China's earlier treaties, since it could, and would be taken by the Powers to imply that Duan, and by association his government, already accepted the pre-existing conditions in Shandong as established by the Twenty-One Demands.

The League of Nations brought into practical politics:
Left to right (seated front row) Viscount Chinda (Japan), next but one, Leon
Bourgeois (France); Lord Robert Cecil; (Great Britain), Vittorio Orlando (Italy);
next but one, Eleftherios Venizelos (Greece).
Second row standing; Colonel House (USA); next but one, Vesnitch (Serbia);
General Smuts (South Africa); President Woodrow Wilson (USA); Paul Hymans
(Belgium); Wellington Koo (China).

II

The Paris Peace Conference

4
Musical Chairs

The autumn of 1918 saw Koo hit by an unexpected tragedy. At the height of the world-wide 'Spanish' flu pandemic, his wife May Tang became one of its victims. She was ill for barely a week, and Koo wrote that: *her death was so sudden that even now I cannot fully convince myself that she has left me forever.*[1]

Despite his grief, Koo was prepared to try any possible tactics to increase his advantage in the forthcoming negotiations. The Chinese delegation at Paris was to have an 'Information Bureau', supposedly to keep journalists apprised of proceedings, but intended from the outset to fight a propaganda war against the Japanese, and to sow doubts between the Americans and British.

Koo's position as a diplomat in America also gave him an opportunity that had been denied many other delegates. Although the Paris Peace Conference did not begin until 1919, Koo was already lobbying the American government in Washington only four days after the Armistice.

On 15 November 1918, Koo called on Robert Lansing, the US Secretary of State, with advanced notice of the Chinese expectations for the Peace Conference. Since Paris was intended to restore peace all over the world, China hoped for the restoration of 'territorial integrity' – those areas that had been stolen from it by foreign aggression. This included the former German lease on Shandong, now under Japanese occupation, and, a claim that was sure to annoy the British, the return of Kowloon in Hong Kong.

In addition, China expected the 'preservation of sovereign rights', the area of Koo's own particular specialisation – the removal of foreign soldiers stationed on Chinese soil, and the abolition of extraterritoriality. Although not stated in such flippant terms in Koo's memorandum, in his idea of a modern China, either Chinese boys would be allowed to cycle on the sidewalk, or English cyclists would be forbidden from doing so – either was fine, but it would be up to the Chinese government to decide and to police, and moreover, to police consistently.

A final demand, for 'fiscal and economic independence', called for the removal of externally imposed trade tariffs – China would make her own rulings regarding taxes on imports and exports.

Lansing passed the buck, or at least waved Koo's comments through without a firm reply, since 11 days later Koo was permitted to make the same comments directly to Woodrow Wilson: *China would hope to present certain proposals at the peace conference concerning her territorial integrity, the preservation of her sovereign rights, and her fiscal and economic independence … merely to restore to her some of the things which, in the view of the Chinese people, had been wrongly taken from her. So the people of China were all looking to the President and the great country which he represented for help in the realization of their just claims and aspirations.*[2]

Koo and Wilson had known each other since Koo's student days. When Koo was still a bright young thing in the overseas Chinese community, Wilson had invited him to dinner during a presidential lecture tour, and had cross-examined him about Chinese attitudes and potential. Koo, then, was at least partly responsible for Wilson's favourable attitude towards China and the Chinese, and the feeling was mutual. Koo was anything but naïve, and it would seem that his meetings with Lansing and Wilson gave him every expectation that America would offer unprecedented support for the Chinese case in Paris.

Wilson also appealed to Koo through his opposition to imperialism. Wilson's Fourteen Points were created in answer to Russian claims about the aims and goals of the Great Powers, and as early as January 1919, Koo was writing excited dispatches to Beijing about the potential for Wilson's putative League of Nations. Wilson's chief aims with the League of Nations were Eurocentric – as with Paris itself, the concerns of the rest of the world were often unwelcome. Koo, however, was unwilling or unable to see this, and instead saw great opportunity in the proposal of a League of Nations. An international body for the settling of international disputes, in which China enjoyed a strong position, was surely an important weapon in the struggle to achieve equal recognition with the Great Powers, and would eventually be termed by Koo *a ray of hope for the oppressed nations in Asia*.[3]

Koo's meeting with Wilson on 26 November 1918 was only for 15 minutes, but it left Koo with the impression that Wilson would do his utmost to support China's case at the Conference. However, even at such an early stage, Wilson was cagey, and noted that 'there were many secret agreements between the subjects of China and other Powers' that were likely to make settlements difficult.[4]

The first signs of trouble came with the selection of the delegates to represent China. While the northern regime in Beijing began to select a five-strong team of delegates, the southern government in Canton selected its own. On 13 December, the southern government put together a strong delegation including Wu Tingfang, former president Sun Yatsen, the American-educated C T Wang, Wu Chaoshu and Wang Jingwei. But the southern government still lacked recognition by the Powers, and did not want to face the inevitable embarrassment of being turned away from the Paris negotiating table. Instead, the south offered Beijing a deal – even though negotiations were still proceeding over rule within China, the country would present a united face in international relations. The mere image of a united China would be a strong bargaining tool in issues over territorial integrity, and defeat many hostile imperialist arguments before they could even be presented. Under pressure from America, Beijing countered with an offer of its own, and the official delegation, representing all China at Paris, took shape.[5]

The nominal leader was Lu Zhengxiang (1871–1949), the former Chinese ambassador to Tsarist Russia. Lu had been baptised soon after birth at the request of his father, who had worked for the London Missionary Society, one of the earliest missionary organisations to work in China. He studied French at a language school that was later incorporated into Beijing's imperial university, and was first assigned to St Petersburg as an interpreter for the Chinese legation – French being the language of choice of the Russian aristocracy. By 1906, he had risen to the rank of counsellor.

Lu's education had already set him in opposition to Chinese tradition, and he lost all faith in the imperial institution in 1896, when his mentor in Russia, Xu Zhingcheng, was recalled to a ministerial post in Beijing. Xu's tenure straddled the Boxer Rebellion and the siege of the Foreign Legations in Beijing, leading Xu to warn Cixi, the Empress Dowager that the Western Powers would avenge themselves on China itself unless she took action. Xu, along with several colleagues, was executed in 1900 for his candour.

Lu Zhengxiang had other motives for remaining in the West. He met and married Berthe Bovy, the daughter of a Belgian military family, who was teaching French in St Petersburg. The wedding took place in St Petersburg's Catholic Church in 1899, and Lu would convert to Catholicism 12 years later. Subsequently, Lu and his new wife were posted to The Hague, where Lu was Minister Plenipotentiary to the Netherlands, and one of the Chinese delegates to the second Hague Peace Conference of 1907. Notably at The Hague, though Lu was part of the delegation, his American adviser, John W Foster, undertook the task of public speaking. Throughout his foreign posting, Lu remained a quiet supporter of Republican China – he cut off his queue in 1902, and on 31 December 1911 joined his fellow leading diplomats in Europe by sending a telegram calling for the abdication of the Last Emperor. With the Emperor still nominally in power, it was a treasonable act, but one that stood Lu in good stead with the proclamation of the Chinese Republic scant weeks later.

Lu's successes abroad, however, were not repeated under the Republic. He was recalled to Beijing to become the Minister of Foreign Affairs, and was appointed Prime Minister in May 1912. Popular legend has it that his opening address to the government was delivered in a Chinese so halting and rusty after over a decade abroad that some ministers instantly regretted their decision. He only held the latter post for a few months, and would resign as Foreign Minister in September

1913 in protest over the government's refusal to ratify a Sino-Russian agreement over Outer Mongolia.

The exhausted Lu and his wife took a prolonged, 18-month 'vacation' in Switzerland, where he undertook a series of ceremonies and presentations on behalf of President Yuan Shikai, who still valued his participation in Chinese diplomacy. Back in China, once again as Foreign Minister, he was in office at the time of the Twenty-One Demands, at which he unsuccessfully attempted to delay negotiations.

After a brief and equally unsuccessful three-month term as Prime Minister again over New Year in 1915/16, Lu was the messenger in Beijing who personally visited each of the Allied envoys in the capital to discuss the terms of China's entry into the war. At the time, he believed that he had secured a deal that China would enter the war on the Allied side, in return for which, the Allied nations would 'agree to a revision of the Chinese tariff, and also the postponement of the Boxer indemnity payout'.[6]

Lu's conciliatory, 'oriental' negotiating style, an inability to answer 'no' to any question, endeared him to the Japanese but infuriated other foreigners. An American State Department official derided him, claiming: '[Lu] has no backbone and needs someone to brace him.' He was also believed by some to be in the pocket of Japan. 'I know [Lu] of old,' wrote Stephen Bonsal of the American delegation, 'and have no confidence in his integrity. He was in 1900 one of the secretaries of [Li Hongzhang] in the ... Boxer negotiations and was known to be open to bribes ... . As a result of previous ... negotiations, the Japanese have a strong hold on him.'[7] Lu even called on the Japanese on his way to France, stopping off in Tokyo for a two-hour meeting with an aggressively expansionist Japanese foreign minister. Lu would later claim that he had acted in China's interests throughout, although the Japanese waved him off to Paris in the belief that he had agreed to cooperate with Japan's demands.

This was certainly the impression Lu had left. When asked in Tokyo: 'The agreements between China and Japan still stand, do they not?' Lu answered with an unequivocal 'Oh yes.' Later arguments at the Peace Conference would break out over whether Lu had meant that he knew they *existed*, or if he acknowledged at that time that they would be honoured.[8]

Lu's standing was not helped in the least by the 'theft' in Tokyo of a box of vital documents from his luggage. By the time he arrived in Paris, the rumour mill was already painting him as a Japanese stooge, in a series of insinuations that would hound him throughout the Conference, and contribute to his declining health.

Lu, at least, was an employee of the same internationally-recognised northern Chinese government as Koo. The northern government had originally intended to send representatives solely of its own choosing, but had been 'persuaded' by Paul Reinsch, the US Minister in China, to include representatives from the south – part of a concerted American effort to add international legitimacy to the southern regime.[9]

The second-in-command of the delegation was therefore C T Wang, the appointee from Sun Yatsen's southern government, whom Koo regarded, at least initially, as a stuffed shirt. Wang was a Yale graduate and hence spoke English, but as far as Koo could see he had little other qualification for a career in international diplomacy. He had served briefly as the Vice Minister of Commerce and Industry in the first Republican cabinet, but since 1918 had been a supporter of the southern regime. C T Wang, in fact, had been in Washington at the time of his appointment to the Peace Conference, lobbying

Wilson to recognise the southern regime as the legitimate government of China, and hence himself as the legitimate Chinese minister in Washington. It was unlikely that he and Koo, the incumbent minister, would be good friends.

Nor was Wang's appointment necessarily welcomed by the southern government, which refused to recognise it – presumably because it was seen less as a political necessity and more an excuse to get him out of Washington. His behaviour was sometimes ill-befitting a diplomat; it was Wang, for example, who had whispered the alleged details of Lu Zhengxiang's Tokyo meeting to the Americans. At the Conference itself, Wang sent a sneaky telegram to the Shanghai newspapers alluding to 'traitors' within his delegation. He may have been joining in the smear campaign against Lu, but could have also been alluding to Koo himself, who, according to Wang, was courting the daughter of the pro-Japanese official Cao Rulin. As events at the Conference would later show, Koo's romantic interests were elsewhere, but the insinuations did not help with the group's hope to present a united front to the rest of the world.

Koo took the third position on the delegation, at his own insistence, in the reasonable expectation that his personal connections with Wilson would prove advantageous. In doing so, he seized a position that should have rightfully belonged to the senior diplomat Alfred Sze (1877–1958), a fellow alumnus of St John's. Sze had also been educated in the United States, at Washington High School and Cornell University, and had been Minister to the Court of St James (Great Britain) since 1914. He was also married to Tang Shaoyi's niece, and hence within the traditional limits of what might be called Koo's own 'family'. Since he still had obligations in London, Sze remained in the background for much of the Conference, as did the final member, Suntchou Wei, the Chinese minister to Belgium. Wei

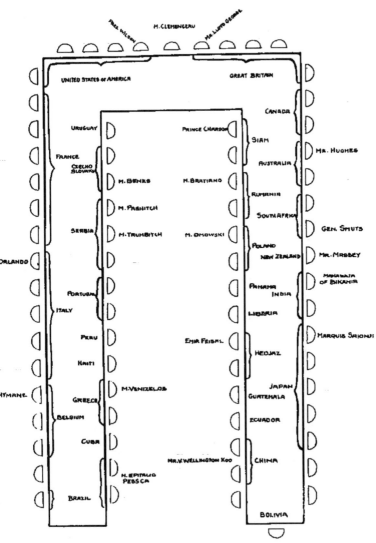

Sketch of the seating plan at the Paris Peace Conference.

played little role in the conference, and was later replaced on the Chinese ticket with C C Wu, Wu Tingfang's son and another southern sinecurist, who arrived late and was similarly invisible at the Conference. Over 50 secretaries and assistants accompanied the main delegates, as well as five foreign advisers, although much of the public work was undertaken by just two people – Lu Zhengxiang and Wellington Koo.

Chief foreign adviser to the Chinese delegation was the ageing Australian adventurer George Morrison (1862–1920). As a medical student, he had begun writing articles during a tour of the South Pacific, walked from Queensland to Melbourne, and later undertook an Asian journey from Shanghai to Rangoon. He became Beijing correspondent for the London *Times* in 1897, and had enjoyed reading his own obituary in the same newspaper after he was believed killed in the Boxer Rebellion. After the 1911 revolution, Morrison quit journalism to become an adviser to the Chinese government. Paris would be his last assignment – he left due to ill health, and died in England soon after.

Morrison was not originally included among the foreign advisers, and fumed in his diary that the Chinese had selected a group of uninformed (and largely forgotten) idiots. 'I praise them highly,' he wrote sarcastically, 'especially de Codt, who was an honest man who knew nothing about China, and was never afraid to say so … his favourite words were "I know nothing" – truthful words. I also praised Denis who equally had the advantage of knowing nothing about China, and as for that oily scoundrel Dr. J.C. Ferguson … I could think of no more fitting representative.'[10]

Allies of Morrison alleged that he was being excluded because of Japanese pressure to keep the delegation weak – an underhand attack on Lu Zhengxiang that probably worked.

Lu soon approached Morrison with the unlikely claim that he was always intended to be chief adviser, but that his appointment needed to remain unofficial to keep a couple of other foreign advisers of equivalent rank, including the Japanese legal expert Ariga Nagao, from expecting to be invited along as well. Morrison, who was already ill, found the entire exercise tiresome, and thought it did not bode well.

The Chinese delegates arrived in Paris and took quarters at the Hotel Lutétia – Morrison was kept at arm's length in the nearby MacMahon Palais. Lu wasted no time in calling for China to have delegates on the three most powerful commissions – he managed to get Wellington Koo onto the commission for the League of Nations, and C T Wang on the meetings discussing International Control of Ports, Railways and Waterways, but failed to get a Chinese presence on the commission discussing International Labour Legislation.

Determined to oil the wheels of diplomacy, Alfred Sze swiftly organised a dinner party on 22 January, to which he invited the British delegation's Ronald Macleay. Wellington Koo and C T Wang also attended, and hence the majority of the Chinese delegation was able to hear, first-hand, of how little interest the British delegation had in supporting China's case. Macleay made no secret of Britain's great debt of gratitude to the Japanese navy, and warned the Chinese that Britain 'could not do much' to help them in the matter of Shandong.[11]

The Chinese arrived expecting five seats at the Conference, but were only assigned two – the seating plan for the full Peace Conference shows all five of their names, but clustered around the same two places as if playing a diplomatic game of musical chairs. Before long, the rivalry between the members reached another level, when Lu received a direct command from Beijing to shuffle the ranks once more. Lu, who was often ill, was sure to be absent from the Conference on several occasions, and Beijing could not abide the thought of C T Wang, an official of an unrecognised regime, taking over as acting leader of the delegation. Consequently, the positions of Wellington Koo and C T Wang were switched. The 32-year-old Koo was now the deputy leader of the entire delegation, but his promotion caused considerable ill feeling with both C T Wang and Alfred Sze. Koo himself pleaded with Lu to reconsider, and apologised to Sze (notably not to Wang) when Lu refused. Sze, however, believed that Koo was only feigning annoyance, and soon sided with Wang in internal arguments within the group.[12] One British observer, lunching with Morrison, compared the Chinese delegation to a circus: 'Self before country is their motto. All intriguing for each other's advancement.'[13]

The Japanese had grievances of their own about their treatment, but still received five seats at the full Conference. Unquestionably, the Chinese had offered a greater material contribution to the war effort, but theirs had been largely invisible to observers who evaluated input in terms of vessels provided or land taken. Whereas the Japanese contribution to the war in Europe had comprised little more than a shipment of marmalade and a desultory number of warships, it was admitted by all sides that the Japanese seizure of German possessions in the Pacific, including Shandong, had freed up a number of Allied troops for the European war effort. But China's contribution was no less great – despite the tragedy of the *Athos*, some 100,000 Chinese labourers were in Europe by the end of 1918, where they had dug and maintained many of the infamous trenches, and done work behind the lines that allowed literally thousands of Allied soldiers to fight.

5
Cat and Mouse

The Japanese were happy to mirror the European powers in their brusque treatment of China. On 26 January 1919, Baron Makino Nobuaki told Associated Press journalists that Japan had 'no territorial interests in China', and that 'if at the Peace Conference Japan was given the right to freely dispose of Qingdao, she will hand it back to China under the terms of the notes exchanged between China and Japan in May, 1915'. This had the desired effect, placing speculation about Japan's benevolent intentions in a number of newspapers over the course of the following week.[1]

Makino's performance behind closed doors before the Council of Ten was entirely different. On 27 January, when the subject of Shandong was first raised, Makino blithely included Shandong in his discussion of other German 'colonies' in the Pacific – a series of small islands that Japan hoped to retain, and in fact, did retain under a series of mandates. The islands were of little interest to any of the powers present, and after some wrangling with the Australians, would eventually end up under a Japanese mandate for the next two decades. In a similar vein, Baron Makino argued that the destruction of the

German naval base in Shandong had been of great value to the Allied cause, and that it was only fitting that Japan should be rewarded with all the rights and possessions in Shandong that had previously belonged to Germany.

Makino's demands were blunt and uncharacteristically direct, and one observer noted that they were spoken with 'a minimum of words, but with very poor delivery'.[2] His arguments also skirted around Japan's real interests in Shandong – the seizure of a territory whose strategic value had been pronounced excellent by Germany.

Makino Nobuaki (1861–1949) was the scion of a prominent family in Japan's southern Satsuma region. A member of Japan's liberal faction, and a supporter of the prominent nobleman Saionji Kinmochi, Makino served as a prefectural governor, a European ambassador (in Italy and Austria) and in ministerial posts during Saionji's administrations. He was a strong supporter of the idea of a League of Nations, and had only agreed to go to Paris if he had his government's backing for the idea. Makino was appointed to the Paris conference at Saionji's insistence, and spoke for Saionji during the early weeks when Saionji was still *en route* to France with other delegates.

The Japanese trick did not work. C T Wang immediately requested an opportunity to respond – Shandong, the size of a European country and with millions of inhabitants, could not be written off quite as easily as a few rocky outcrops in the Pacific, particularly when it rightfully belonged to a fellow ally. With time running on, China was given leave to respond the following day.[3]

As soon as the meeting was over, Koo called on Wilson, ostensibly to introduce him to Lu Zhengxiang. In fact, it was a thinly disguised excuse to talk over the day's events, and Wilson was quick to note his surprise at Makino's behaviour. Makino had, he thought, been remarkably naïve in the presentation of his case, and Wilson urged Koo to hold nothing back in his response. Wilson agreed to 'try' to enlist British support for the Shandong case, but warned Koo once again that the British alliance with Japan would make such a task difficult. Koo pressed for something a little more substantial, asking Wilson if he might consider making a personal statement on the record in support of the Chinese case. Wilson's reply was non-committal: he 'felt deeply sympathetic to China and would do his best to help her'.[4]

Although Koo was not aware of it, his presence had intimidated the Japanese and left them scrambling for explanations. Baron Makino had arrived in Paris believing that Japan's interests in China had already been settled; indeed, he had been assured of such the previous day, in a brief conversation with Lu Zhengxiang. But when Makino had arrived before the Council of Ten, Lu was nowhere in sight. Makino came to believe that Koo and Wang had organised some sort of internal revolution against Lu. Moreover, he noted that several of the Chinese delegates' phrases and wordings seemed too close to those of the American Lansing for comfort; Makino believed that despite the lack of official American advisers to the Chinese delegation, the Chinese nevertheless had unofficial American assistance. Koo was, after all, on friendly terms with Wilson, and had even been spotted swapping college reminiscences and even singing Columbia songs with members of the American delegation. Believing that the Americans and the Chinese were secretly united against him, Makino leaned on Britain and France, both of whom offered assurances that they would support Japan.[5]

Makino's suspicions were only partly justified. It is possible that he may have missed a far more important element in support of the Chinese in Paris. With the ailing Lu Zhengxiang out of the way, the Chinese delegation presented a public face of youth and vitality, and many of them had rich and varied contacts with the American delegates. Koo was by no means the only Chinese diplomat with old friends among the US delegates and advisers.

'The Chinese at Paris,' commented Ray Stannard Baker, 'were practically all American or British educated, and spoke English fluently. They were much more open, outright and frank than the Japanese.' Another American delegate, having been sumptuously entertained by the Chinese at the Hotel Lutétia, commented that his hosts were dignified, largely educated to a doctoral level, and 'none over fifty'. Without a doubt, the Chinese beat the Japanese hands down at making friends.[6]

The meeting of the Council of Ten on 28 January was a momentous event for Asian affairs. It was the only occasion at the Conference where Japan and China argued face-to-face before the Great Powers, and the precise wording of its minutes would be the cause of endless subsequent debates. It contained revelations over secret treaties that would colour all future discussion of China's case. It was also the first time that Wellington Koo spoke before an international congress.

Koo's relationship with Wilson was a prime factor in pushing him to the fore on 28 January. Although the Great Powers did not know it at the beginning of the day, he was also intimately acquainted with the secret negotiations over Shandong, having personally worked on many of the drafts. He also had a certain propaganda value. The other delegates had heard Japan's case presented in a halting, bluff manner by Makino. On the morning of the 28th, Koo began his speech with an understandable tremor in his voice. But before long, he hit them with the full force of an American education, and his long history of public speaking and debating society medals.

'Wellington Koo,' wrote Clemenceau, was 'like a young Chinese cat, Parisian of speech and dress, absorbed in the pleasure of patting and pawing the mouse, even if it was reserved for the Japanese.'[7]

Koo pointed out that the Germans should not have been in Shandong in the first place, and topped his argument by citing the Peace Conference's own agreed tenets of nationality and territorial integrity, and by shrewdly alluding to issues that would make more sense to a European audience. Shandong was, said Koo, *the cradle of Chinese civilization, the birthplace of Confucius and Mencius, and a Holy Land for the Chinese.*

> Wellington Koo [was] like a young Chinese cat ... absorbed in the pleasure of patting and pawing the mouse, even if it was reserved for the Japanese.
> **GEORGES CLEMENCEAU**

It was also, he said, refusing to pretend that the Japanese had no strategic interests, and playfully reversing Japan's former strategic assessment, *a dagger pointed at the heart of China.*[8]

In a debating tactic that had been part of his victories in his student days, Koo began by pretending to agree with his opponents, acknowledging their 'assistance' before hitting them with a sarcastic reversal. Yes, he agreed, the Japanese had 'helped' retake Shandong, but so had the British and all the other Allies, each in their own way. And come to mention it, the Chinese had hardly sat idly by themselves: *China was fully cognizant of the services rendered to her by the heroic army and navy of Japan in rooting out German power from [Shandong]. China was also deeply indebted to Great Britain for helping in this task at a time of great peril to herself in Europe. China was also not forgetful of the services rendered her by the troops of the other Allies in Europe which had held*

*in check an enemy who might otherwise have easily sent rein-
forcements to the Far East and thereby prolonging hostilities
there. China appreciated these services all the more because
her people in [Shandong] had also suffered and sacrificed in
connection with the military operations for the capture of
[Jiaozhou], especially in regard to requisitions for labour and
supplies of all kinds.*

But, Koo reasoned, this was supposedly an enlightened
age, not a 19th-century scramble for land and wealth. None
of the above presented an excuse for Chinese territory to
be handed to a third party. It belonged to the Chinese, and
they would be pleased to have it back: *But grateful as they
were, the Chinese delegation felt that they would be false in
their duty to China and to the world if they did not object
to paying their debts of gratitude by selling the birthright of
their countrymen and thereby sowing the seeds of discord for
the future. The Chinese delegation therefore trusted that the
Conference, in considering the disposal of the leased territory and other rights held by Germany in [Shandong], would
give full weight to the fundamental and transcendent rights
of China, the rights of political sovereignty and territorial
integrity as well as her earnest desire to serve the cause of
universal peace.*[9]

Koo alluded to China's position in previous years, when it
had been forced behind the scenes to sign treaties against its
will, most notably the awful settlements of the Twenty-One
Demands.

'When Koo presented himself before the Council of Ten,'
wrote Lu Zhengxiang, 'he was astounded to hear Mr Lloyd
George put a question to him: "The Twenty-One Demands
– what's that?"'[10]

The cat was out of the bag. Japan's backdoor bullying was

now a matter of public record. Although the Council did not seek further explanation at the time, it would soon become apparent that the Chinese had been acting under duress in the signing of many treaties that the outside world had assumed were voluntary. The matter of secret pressure on China would become a fundamental part of the ensuing debate, and Koo had introduced it at his earliest opportunity.

Koo's speech was a triumph. It quite literally put China on the map for many of the previously uninterested delegates. It made the Japanese out to be the very belligerent bullies that the Chinese information bureau had been suggesting all along, and in presenting a youthful, eloquent face to the world, Koo had scored an immense victory for China on the world stage. In the aftermath, Koo was surrounded by well-wishers offering appreciation. Even Clemenceau, who had sat silent throughout the Shandong debate, approached Koo afterwards and passed on his secret congratulations – which, inevitably, were soon known all over Paris. It took literally months for the Japanese to muster an appropriate rebuttal, in the form of a sarcastic comment by Chinda Sutemi, who observed belatedly in April: 'Does it not seem strange to you that the Japanese forces driving the Germans out of the holy province of Confucius did not receive the support of a single Chinaman?' [11] By then, of course, it was too late – Koo's victory, at least in the opening debate, was a matter of record.

'As if by some sort of magic,' wrote Koo's secretary, Wunsz King, 'his fame as a youthful diplomatist spread all over China overnight … a large section of the population deluded themselves with the vague idea that triumph at the Conference table was almost around the corner.' But not even Koo's performance at the Peace Conference united all the Chinese – even within his own government at home, a faction remained that was intensely distrustful of the Peace Conference, and that continued to favour direct negotiations with the Japanese in a specifically Asian solution. This faction would only remain quiet and powerless for as long as Koo and his fellow delegates scored points in Paris.[12]

On 2 February 1919, the Japanese minister Obata Torikichi paid a call on China's acting Minister of Foreign Affairs in Beijing to complain, in particular, about Koo's unauthorised disclosure of the secret agreements between China and Japan. Although Obata did not specifically threaten military action, he was sure to allude to half a million tons of Japanese navy, a million Japanese soldiers, and asked what friends the Chinese thought they had. He also raised a technical issue – a Chinese government bureau had recently changed its name, which, if one wanted to be bloody-minded over contracts, would invalidate some previous paperwork and obligate China to renegotiate its war loans or face having to pay Japan back in one huge payment.

China caved in, and timidly agreed not to disclose any of the details of the secret agreements without Japan's prior permission. This, perhaps, helps to explain why Lu Zhengxiang claimed his papers had been 'stolen', since otherwise he could have simply walked them over to the Conference by hand.

Nor did Koo's performance win him any friends in his own delegation – he may have even introduced Lu Zhengxiang to Wilson out of a sense of guilt, having been mistaken by the rest of those present for the leader of the Chinese. Alfred Sze threatened to resign if Koo continued to push himself ahead of his rightful superiors, and C T Wang continued his whispering campaign regarding Koo's supposed romantic interest in Cao Rulin's daughter.

The subject of Shandong, however, was swiftly set aside in favour of more pressing matters, leaving both the Chinese and Japanese to plot their next move in the intervening weeks. Koo's speech had publicly broached the subject of secret deals between the Chinese and Japanese, and the Japanese and other Great Powers, leading Wilson to call for the Japanese to reveal their contents. In the weeks that followed, as more details came out of the northern Chinese government's appeasement of Japan, the southern delegates, most notably C T Wang, became increasingly critical of the north, and by association, their own leader, Lu Zhengxiang.

Beneath the notice of most at Paris, a separate Shanghai Peace Conference commenced in February 1919, between representatives of the northern and southern governments of China. Shanghai achieved little in itself, but served to concentrate Chinese attention on the concerns of Paris, and the news that was escaping from Paris of previous betrayals. Sun Yatsen, as the leader of the southern Chinese, was scathing towards the northern regime's damaging deals with the Japanese. Talk of the Twenty-One Demands was all over the press, leading the American Minister to China, Paul Reinsch, to send a message to his superiors outlining the problems of the 'secret agreements'. He suggested, among other things, that 'the [Paris] Peace Conference insists upon the submission of all agreements whatsoever and with whomsoever the Chinese Government [made them] during the war, including military agreements and so-called industrial matters such as the telephone, [Jilin] forestry and [Fujian] loans. All agreements not submitted ought to be considered ipso facto invalid'.[13]

Behind the scenes in Paris, the Great Powers were getting tired of waiting. Koo had claimed that Japan had made a number of secret and unlawful deals with China. The Great

Powers had asked to see them. The Chinese had agreed to bring them along, and then suddenly 'lost' them. Hoping that the Shandong Question would crawl away and die, the British and American delegations suggested, seemingly off the record, to Lu Zhengxiang that China and Japan should take it off the table at Paris, and sort it out among themselves. This was soon reported to Beijing, where the Chinese President was justifiably concerned. He in turn called on Paul Reinsch, who threw the matter back in the American's delegation's faces.

Reinsch sent an urgent cable to Lansing, pointing out how pointless such a decision would be. Reinsch boldly alluded to a suspicion that was already gaining ground among the Chinese, that Wilson was going to sell them out. 'I hesitate to believe that it is the intention to hand [Shandong] rights over to Japan, as would be the result of referring them for settlement to Japan and China. The Chinese government at present is not representative and is not able to resist any suggestion of Japan. Such fundamental matters ... should be reserved for mature decision after considering the rights of the Chinese people and other nations.' [14]

Diplomatically but clearly, Reinsch had predicted the central, inevitable consequence of the Shandong Question. If the Powers could not even settle the question of Shandong, then what was the point of a League of Nations?

Lansing's reply of 28 February slapped Reinsch's concerns down, and stopped just short of calling him a liar. 'The Chinese delegation informs me that it has not received any such advice from the American or the British delegation.'

Meanwhile, the Japanese lost further ground with the Great Powers at the Peace Conference through their dogged pursuit of a 'racial equality' clause in the charter of the League of Nations. Although regarded by some as an innocuous and harmless statement, it had unwelcome implications for several nations – particularly the Americans and the Australians, with a fear of Japanese immigration, and the British, with a colonial hold on India.

Koo's press office continued a propaganda campaign against the Japanese, which continued to reap benefits, both in public support, and in anger among the Japanese delegation. Stephen Bonsal was not surprised. Despite his dislike of the Japanese, he wrote: 'every broken-down newspaperman from the east coast of Asia is here writing scurrilous articles about the Japanese ... The Chinese should recover [Shandong] and I have no doubt that they will, but it would be much easier to persuade the Japanese to take this proper step if the Chinese press would refrain from its campaign of abuse.'

As far as Bonsal was concerned, the Chinese had 'spent millions in publicity to prove that the Japanese army is a big bad wolf and a menace to the peace of the world – which everybody knew'. He was not alone in thinking that the Chinese smear campaign had only served to alienate reasonable Japanese diplomats, and made the Chinese case more difficult to pursue.[15]

Koo met with Wilson on 26 March, when the US President continued to reassure him that he had China's best interests in mind. They met yet again on 17 April, after which Koo prepared a long memo for Wilson's assistants. Wilson himself read the document, but offered no comments beyond his thanks. Koo's memo reiterated, with some force, his belief that America was China's friend. It also pointed out that Shandong was not merely an issue of vital importance to China's political independence, territorial integrity and economic welfare, but that it was also crucial to foreign powers:

[Qingdao], being the best harbour on the coast of China and connected as it is, by a system of railways, with the principal centres of production and distribution, is destined to control ... the entire trade of North China. To leave the port or the ... railway in the hands of any foreign power, is, therefore, to place in its hands the most powerful weapon for securing trade domination and for jeopardizing the principle of equal opportunities for the commerce of all nations.[16]

Koo also pressed for the issue to be resolved by the Peace Conference, and not through private agreement between China and Japan, as the latter course would *imply a recognition of the Treaties and Notes which Japan compelled China to accept*, one of which bound China to agree to any deal made between Japan and Germany. Koo conceded that France, Britain and Italy had all given assurances to Japan that they would support its claims over Shandong, but also noted that they had done so when China was not an ally. He called on America to overrule the previous deals, noting, with a cunning flourish, that the deals were invalid under the terms of Wilson's Fourteen Points anyway. Finally, Koo suggested that returning Shandong was also in Japan's interests, as it would prove that Japan really was as interested in China's welfare as the nation so often claimed.

Perhaps in an effort to demonstrate that China was prepared to play fair if Japan would too, Koo even offered tentative support to a Japanese motion. When the subject of racial equality came up again on 11 April, Koo produced a very carefully worded statement that: *I believe that the principle contained in the Japanese amendment involves a number of questions to which time alone can give a universally satisfactory solution. Nevertheless I should be very glad indeed to see the principle itself given recognition in the Covenant, and I hope that the Commission will not find serious difficulties in the way of its acceptance.*[17]

Shandong was back on the agenda on 22 April, at a meeting of France, the US and the UK (the 'Big Three') where Wilson lamented the number of secret treaty engagements between Japan and China, and Japan, Britain and France. Lloyd George, who supposedly had not even heard of the Twenty-One Demands until that day, put an exasperated question to Koo: 'Which would China prefer – to allow Japan to succeed to the German rights in [Shandong] as stated in the treaty between China and Germany, or to recognize Japan's position in [Shandong] as stipulated in the treaties between China and Japan?'[18]

Whatever Lloyd George's motives may have been, the question sounded to Koo like an ultimatum. Koo answered delicately that *both alternatives were unacceptable.* As the afternoon wore on, the presentation of the notes of agreements between the Chinese and Japanese seemed to persuade Lloyd George that he had spoken out of turn, and that Koo had been right to argue that China had been forced to sign treaties against its will with an untrustworthy ally. Lloyd George offered Koo a form of apology, and suggested that Great Britain, even as an ally of Japan, could not be bound to support an agreement which had been made 'behind their back' as a result of the Twenty-One Demands. By this time, however, Wilson appears to have seized upon Lloyd George's unanswerable question. He had already observed earlier in the afternoon that the Powers 'were bound to keep these treaties because the war has largely been fought for the purpose of showing that treaties cannot be violated'. Not recorded in the minutes, but noted by one of the Chinese present was an even stronger assertion from Wilson: 'It would be better to live up to a bad treaty than to tear it [up].'[19]

Consequently, even though Lloyd George appeared to have a change of heart, Wilson repeated the question to Koo: Would China rather keep her agreement with Japan than allow Japan to succeed to the German position in Shandong?

Koo's reply was not a threat, but a simple statement of the facts. *If ... they did not get justice, China might be driven into the arms of Japan. There was a small section in China which believed in Asia for the Asiatics and wanted the closest cooperation with Japan alone. The position of the Government, however, was that they believed in the justice of the West and that their future lay there.*

Koo argued that the 'treaties' under discussion were unjust because they had been made under wartime conditions which China had subsequently invalidated by joining hostilities herself, effectively on the same side as Japan. Moreover, the Allies themselves had now adopted new principles as the basis of peace, principles which Japan was now contravening. Koo finished by stating *the importance of attaining a peace which could be relied upon to endure for fifty years, instead of a peace so unjust that it would only sow the seeds of early discord.*[20]

Wilson gave an uneasy reply, centred on the pre-existence of the treaties between China and Japan, which he could not readily overrule. In fact, 'the sacredness of treaties had been one of the motives of the war'. The Peace Conference could not simply tear up those treaties that were now inconvenient.

Yes, said Koo, but surely it was better to unravel those problems now that would otherwise ruin the prospective future of the peace they were trying to establish. Now Lloyd George stepped in, reminding the council that he had a treaty of his own with Japan, which he, too, was obliged to honour.

Regardless of whether or not Britain could have captured Jiaozhou without Japanese help, 'Great Britain could not turn round to Japan now and say "All right, thank you very much, when we wanted your help, you gave it, but we now think the treaty was a bad one and should not be carried out".' [21]

Lloyd George ended by suggesting that he was in favour of welcoming China to the League of Nations, and helping the country against oppression. But, he added, joining the international community also implied abiding by its codes of conduct, and that also applied to pre-existing treaties.

> China is now at the parting of the ways. She has come to the West for justice. If she should fail to get it, the people would attribute the failure ... to the attitude of the West ...
>
> **WELLINGTON KOO**

If Koo was hoping for an ounce of help from Clemenceau, it was not forthcoming. The French leader, already bored beyond belief, grumbled that he agreed with whatever Lloyd George had said, implying in the process that he had not really been listening.

China is now at the parting of the ways, wrote a dejected Koo that night. *She has come to the West for justice. If she should fail to get it, the people would attribute the failure ... to the attitude of the West which declined to lend a helping hand to China merely because some its leading Powers had privately pledged to support Japan.* [22]

On 24 April, Baron Makino called on the American delegation, and announced that he would not be signing the Treaty unless the Conference accepted his informal promise to return Shandong, and the principle that Japan would enjoy the benefit of unequal treaties in Shandong identical to those already enjoyed by the Western Powers. 'In Tokyo,' he said, 'they do not seem to see why we should be the least-favoured nation in our relations with [Shandong] simply because almost unaided, with but the nominal support of a British token force, we rescued the province from the German invaders.'

The following day, the Japanese offered a memorandum that appeared to offer the Chinese a deal. After beginning with a plaintive assertion that this had all been more or less worked out amicably in Tokyo by Lu Zhengxiang before the Peace Conference had even begun, and that there was no need for any 'malicious reports', the memo went on: 'We are prepared to return to China the territory of [[Jiaozhou], which we took from Germany at considerable expenditure of men and treasure. We are turning it back to China eighty years before the lease the Chinese gave the Germans expires, which we took over from the Germans by right of conquest. In appreciation of this step we ask the Chinese to give us commercial opportunities in [Shandong] equal to those which the other foreign powers now enjoy, no more, no less.'[23]

The Japanese proposal received the support of Clemenceau and Balfour, but was met with fury by the Chinese delegation. Despite being couched in language that implied everything was being done to Chinese satisfaction, the offer still violated principle by 'returning' Chinese territory from Germany to Japan, and was entirely vague about when Japan might deign to hand Shandong back, and could be read in one sense as an entirely voluntary move, which Japan might later abrogate.

An anonymous manifesto, written by someone with an intimate understanding of the deals made and advice heard, circulated in Paris in multiple languages at the beginning of May. Bonsal believed it to be the work of the Chinese delegation, and specifically Koo himself. The document claimed, among other things: 'After nibbling at the question for weeks, the Big Four turned the matter over to Mr Balfour, a surprising ineptitude, as he is the sponsor if not the father of the Anglo-Japanese Alliance.'[24] China, it said, had been 'stabbed in the heart in the house of its friends'.

George Morrison, adviser to the Chinese, was preparing to leave Paris, ill with jaundice, but took the time to tell the Americans that the Chinese felt directly betrayed by Wilson, who had so diligently assured them that he would support their case. They had trusted Wilson's claim that they could 'rely on him', he said, 'and now we are betrayed in the house of our only friend' – a telling paraphrase of the anonymous essay.

American advisers were similarly irate. E T Williams, from the State Department, noted disconsolately to Bonsal that the Japanese were only 'returning' Jiaozhou. They were keeping the railway across the whole peninsula, and the mines. Williams was aghast that the Peace Conference had let such a deception occur and likened the Great Powers to a bungling sheriff: 'Now the policeman comes along, rebukes the robber, but allows him to keep the stolen property.'[25]

6
Days of Sorrow

Sunday 4 May 1919 is remembered in China as a momentous day in history, although in Paris it was of no obvious importance. In a rush to complete its mission on time, the Council of Four sent the German treaty to be printed. Lloyd George went off for a picnic, while everyone else simply idled at their residences. It was hoped that the Treaty would be signed swiftly, bringing the arguments to an end. In fact, the Treaty was not signed until 28 June, on a bright summer's day at the lavishly decorated Hall of Mirrors in the Palace of Versailles.

The finalisation for the printers of what would become the Treaty of Versailles meant, of course, that there could be no more changes. The wrangles over Shandong were now frozen in their previous state, with no hope of alteration. It was not long before the decision over Shandong, widely seen as an American 'betrayal', was known in Beijing. Student radicals, many of whom had enthusiastically supported stronger ties with the West, were now sufficiently disenchanted to turn on their allies. Representatives of 13 different universities and institutions of higher education in the Chinese capital, numbering some 3,000, met in the afternoon of 4 May in a mass protest in front of Beijing's Gate of Heavenly Peace (Tiananmen). The slogans chanted included rejections of the Twenty-One Demands, refusal to sign the Treaty of Versailles and, ominous calls for 'punishment' of those who had betrayed China's interests abroad. In the ensuing riot, the mob set fire to the house of Cao Rulin, the pro-Japanese Minister of Communications, and seriously assaulted Zhang Zong-xiang, the Minister to Tokyo. There were further casualties on the side of the students, with many injuries and one death.

Frank L Polk, the Acting US Secretary of State, could already see the damage being done by the decision. On 4 May, he cabled Lansing with a stern suggestion that Wilson make some sort of public statement to allay the fears of the Chinese people. Polk genuinely feared not only that America would lose standing with the Chinese, but that the Chinese would turn on their own representatives in Paris, blaming Koo and C T Wang for decisions that they had resolutely tried to prevent. With that in mind, Polk urged Wilson to say something in support of China, and also in praise of the work of Koo and Wang, so that it 'might help to solidify the national sentiment and prevent any further factional manifestations'.[1] Lansing took the idea to Wilson, who agreed in principle to say something suitable, as long as Lansing would write it for him. There is no evidence that the proclamation was ever drafted, and the idea was lost amidst the whirl of other Conference duties.

Resentment also spread among Chinese students studying abroad, some of who were embarrassingly available to cause trouble in Paris itself. A meeting on 5 May to discuss Chinese affairs resulted in a 'near-riot', with Chinese students studying in Paris haranguing the American representatives, and even making open threats against Wilson and his 'Japanese friends'. Stephen Bonsal, who was present, was shocked to see that even the women, led by the art student Emilie Tcheng, were calling for direct action: 'We must stop preaching peace. We must go in for force.'[2]

The unrest at home and abroad was enough to spook the ongoing sessions of the Shanghai Peace Conference. With little success in their own deliberations over north-south rapprochment, the Shanghai delegates instead turned their anger towards foreign affairs, cabling Paris on 6 May with an uncompromising warning: 'In case the Peace Conference should accede to the demand of another Power [Japan], while ignoring our claim, the four hundred million people of China, in the name of justice and righteousness, would never agree to such a decision. We request that you do not sign the treaty … '[3] The message was all the stronger for being signed by representatives of both northern and southern governments. The southern signatory was Tang Shaoyi, the father of Wellington Koo's late wife.

The people of Shandong were even more direct, holding a Conference for Commemoration of National Humiliation, at which some 30,000 attendees supposedly ratified a resolution protesting against the Paris decision. The Shandong representatives dispatched their own telegram to the Chinese delegation in Paris, stating: 'If you sign any treaty which includes a clause that Japan has any rights in [Shandong], we shall subject you to the same treatment as has been meted out to Zhang and Cao when you return.'[4]

The 4 May protests were a watershed. China's disillusionment with the West created a fad for 'modernisation' that sought to sweep away everything tainted with thoughts of the past – it led to the repudiation of Confucianism, and a 'New Culture Movement' that sought to make knowledge available to the masses through a simplification of literary Chinese. The May Fourth Movement, as it became known, formed the basis of what was to become the Chinese Communist Party, as intellectuals sought an alternative to the betrayed expectations of Paris. The Peace Conference, and Wilson's Fourteen Points, the Great Powers, the United States and Europe, had had their chances, and had let the Chinese down. Instead, the Chinese turned to new inspiration, which they would eventually find in Soviet Russia. But at the time such protests took place, the concerns of all at Paris were more personal in nature – Koo and his associates were worried that they would become the next victims.

In return for giving up Shandong, the best the Powers could offer the Chinese was a paltry concession. Enshrined in Article 131 of the Treaty of Versailles is the earnest note that Germany should return to China a set of valuable large-scale astronomical instruments that had been looted from the Beijing Observatory during the Boxer Rebellion. Tucked further down the Treaty, at Articles 156–8, is the handing over of Shandong from Germany to Japan; an area the size of a European nation, even down to its railways and submarine cables, was swapped for a handful of sextants and astrolabes.[5]

On 9 May, Wellington Koo spent an hour with American delegates, and announced he would only sign the treaty if Beijing ordered him to; and even then, he would do so in the expectation that he was signing his own death warrant. His sometime superior Lu Zhengxiang was in hearty agreement.

'For the first time in my life,' wrote Lu, 'I believed it to be my duty not to obey ... I was not willing to sign my name yet again to unjust clauses, and I took it upon myself alone to refuse my signature.'[6]

The Chinese delegates were not alone in their opposition. From Beijing, Paul Reinsch cabled his superiors a long document on 23 May that showed a series of glaring omissions in the ruling on Shandong. What possible logic was there, asked Reinsch, in handing Japan all of Shandong, when the country's forces had only occupied the city of Jiaozhou and the railway – in essence, the Peace Conference was helping Japan to acquire further territory, supposedly because Japan already occupied it, although in truth Japan did not.

Furthermore, argued Reinsch, the Japanese were being given preferential rights in Shandong, as if they had simply taken over the German concessions in the area. But the German concessions had been terminated with the Chinese declaration of war on Germany in 1917. There were, then, no German preferential rights remaining for the Japanese to take over.

By this time, Reinsch had a copy of the draft of the Treaty of Versailles, in which he noted further loopholes that the Japanese were sure to exploit. According to the draft Treaty, Japan was to get everything that Germany had had in Shandong, without any restrictions or obligations imposed on Japan. And yet, even in the original treaty of 1898 between Germany and China, it was stated that China retained sovereignty over Shandong.

Reinsch was deeply concerned at the precedent set by the Treaty of Versailles. Germany's original deal with China, right or wrong, had been simply between the two states. Japan's seizure of Shandong was now being ratified and acknowledged by the entire international community at the Peace Conference. Moreover, Reinsch was ready to believe that

Shandong was only the thin end of the wedge, and that once Japan was safely in its new concession, it would make further demands and impositions on the Chinese. 'If the [Shandong] settlement is approved in the form in which it stands in the peace treaty,' wrote Reinsch, ' ... the situation created will be unfavourable to the prospects of maintaining peace in the Far East and distinctly adverse to the best interests of the United States.'[7]

Reinsch's complaints fell on deaf ears. A month later on 7 June, citing 'nearly six years of continuous strain,' he resigned as the American minister to China. Although Shandong was not his sole reason, his resignation was certainly coloured by recent events. His resignation letter to Wilson noted the dangers presented by the military regime in Tokyo, and warned that there were already signs that America was next on Japan's hitlist: 'If this force, with all the methods it is accustomed to apply, remains unopposed, there will be created in the Far East the greatest engine of military oppression and dominance that the world has yet seen. Not can we avoid the conclusion that the brunt of evil results will fall on the United States, as is already foreshadowed by the bitter hostility and abnormal vituperativeness of the Japanese press with regard to America.'[8]

> If [Japan], with all the methods it is accustomed to apply, remains unopposed, there will be created in the Far East the greatest engine of military oppression and dominance that the world has yet seen.
>
> **PAUL REINSCH**

Since even the American advisers had their doubts about the Shandong settlement, it is unsurprising that Wellington Koo made one final attempt to push for signing the Treaty of Versailles with reservations on 24 June. He first asked if it would be possible to simply add reservations about Shandong to his signature on the document. When this was ruled out, he suggested instead that there be an annex to the Treaty, setting out Chinese conditions. This, too was refused. Under instructions from Beijing not to sign without reservations, Koo tried instead to redefine the term. He offered to sign the Treaty, but only after being allowed to make a separate declaration, entirely divorced from the text of the Treaty itself, that the Shandong question should be reconsidered at a future date.[9]

Not even this fallback position met with approval from the other delegates, who were worried about the precedent it might set for encouraging other signatories to opt out of clauses they did not like. Koo, always ready with unwelcome facts, replied that the precedent was already set, in the Treaty of Vienna in 1815, which the Swedes had been permitted to sign with reservation. The last straw came when someone suggested that Germany might also like to avail itself of the chance to sign with reservations. Curtly reminding the council that China had been an Allied Power and not an enemy, Koo left the room. In his absence, Clemenceau predictably threw out the idea of any single signatory opting out of any particular clauses.

Neither Koo nor Lu could bring themselves to put their names to a document that had ignored justice for their country. In fact, in Beijing, it was unclear who was empowered to issue orders to the Paris delegation one way or the other. Pro-Japanese ministers in the Beijing government had been forced to resign in the wake of the 4 May protests, leaving the Chinese President, Xu Shichang, nominally in charge. But when Lu and Koo cabled him for confirmation, the President himself tried to resign rather than offer a reply that might cause difficulties. The Prime Minister, Xu's subordinate, was himself replaced on 13 June, and a new cabinet sworn in on 23 June, less than a week before the Treaty of Versailles was due to be signed.

The delegates in Paris waited anxiously for notification from the new cabinet, but a confirmation one way or the other was still unforthcoming. As 28 June loomed, the Chinese delegates were forced to decide for themselves. Unanimously, they agreed that they could not sign the Treaty of Versailles. Instead, Koo and his fellow delegates issued a press release, the vocabulary and tone of which seem to have been largely the work of Koo.

'The Peace Conference having denied China justice in the settlement of the Shandong question, and having today in effect prevented them from signing the treaty without sacrificing their sense of right, justice and patriotic duty, the Chinese delegates submit their case to the impartial judgement of the world.' [10]

Koo walked alone in the streets of Paris, musing that 28 June 1919 *must remain in the history of China as the day of sorrow*.[11] A measure of comfort arrived, late as ever, when the sun was setting over the Hall of Mirrors. As Lu remembered: 'In the evening of that very same day, very late, when the closing session of the Conference had come to an end several hours before, an entirely unexpected telegram from my Government gave me the counter-order which I had had the boldness to carry out of my own accord.' [12] After the fact, Koo and the other delegates now enjoyed the support of their own government.

Many in the international community continued to regard the Chinese stance with bafflement. The London *Times* earnestly expressed hope that the Japanese would soon restore Shandong as an act of goodwill. This however, was part of

China's objection – Koo and his fellow delegates refused to rely upon the goodwill of an aggressor to return territory that rightfully belonged to China. It was, as Koo's secretary Wunsz King noted archly, 'like negotiating with a tiger for its skin'.

The deadlock also left China still technically at war with Germany; a side-effect that would be quietly cleared up in the 1920s. However, since Koo and his fellow delegates did not have similar objections about other treaties that formed part of the Peace Conference, China was a willing signatory to the Treaty of Neuilly with Bulgaria, and the Treaty of Trianon with Hungary. There was a minor spat on 12 July over the Treaty of St Germain with Austria, when Italy demanded that property that had been formerly held in the Chinese city of Tianjin by Austria-Hungary should be ceded to the Italian government. It was a minor issue, hardly a territorial dispute and more like a request for the Italian concession to extend its boundaries in order to deal with some swampy ground and gain better river access – they had asked for the boundary change before, in 1917. However, Koo refused to admit the thin end of such a wedge – there could only be further damage to the Treaty of Versailles if Austria's portion was not returned to China. Instead, China agreed to improve drainage in the area, to make life easier for the Italians.

There were also some wrangles over what had once been Austria-Hungary's portion of the Boxer Indemnity, which the new state of Austria hoped to continue to receive. This was slapped down by the Supreme Council, allowing China to sign the Treaty of St Germain with a small victory – some special privileges once enjoyed by the Germans and Austrians in China were now cancelled.[13]

In hindsight, Koo's secretary Wunsz King thought that the

Americans had tried to do their best by China, and could not be blamed for their failure. In fact, King still believed that the Chinese owed Wilson a 'debt of gratitude' for his heroic efforts. In King's opinion, the traitor was Lloyd George, whose dogged adherence to the secret and questionable treaties between Britain and Japan had not allowed any room for compromise. King felt that a more flexible approach from Lloyd George would have given Wilson better room for compromise, and, since Clemenceau had deferred to Lloyd George at every decisive juncture on Shandong, would have ensured stronger French support as well.[14]

Objectively, some of the blame should also be laid at the feet of the Chinese, although the inability to point to a responsible Chinese party was also part of the problem. The Chinese delegates had performed admirably, but had suffered through their inexperience and through the inevitable conflicts over seniority caused by the arguments between China's two rival governments. Lu Zhengxiang had arrived in Paris already pessimistic about China's chances, and had not made much effort to put his fluent French to use persuading the French themselves to offer more active support. Lu had already given up, and although he was nominally appointed as the Chinese ambassador to Switzerland, he was effectively retired from Paris onwards, and would later become a Catholic monk in Belgium.

Democrats might even seek a silver lining among the clouds. The Paris Peace Conference was the first time that the speed of modern communications allowed the Chinese people to monitor the activities of their representatives abroad in something close to real time. Although the Chinese delegation failed in its mission, and the attention of Chinese citizens often seemed more like mob rule, it was at least an opportunity for the mob to make itself heard. Koo and his fellow delegates refused to sign the Treaty of Versailles because of their fear of reprisals from the Chinese people themselves – for the first time, the voice of the Chinese people was discernible above that of a minority of politicians and aristocrats, even if it clamoured for reprisals.

Furthermore, the Japanese victory in Paris destroyed the power of the pro-Japanese faction in Beijing. Japanese-educated and Japan-supported politicians in China lost credibility, affording faster career paths for the Anglo-American faction represented by the likes of Wellington Koo. Even though he had 'failed' in Paris, he had done so heroically, and that alone would buy him a chance to right some of the wrongs of the Treaty of Versailles.

7

Marriage in Haste

Koo might have taken some solace from the news that his feelings on Shandong were shared by many Americans, were it not for the damage that this news was doing to the Treaty of Versailles as a whole. Senators in Washington queued up to denounce the Shandong deal, using forceful rhetoric that spoke of the rape of China, the immorality of the settlement, and repeatedly spoke of theft and robbery. Senator William Borah, an opponent of the League of Nations who gained the nickname of 'the Lion of Idaho', delivered the most stinging of rebukes to Wilson, calling the deal: 'So immoral and unrighteous that we wish to approach it with deaf ears and closed eyes ... It will dishonour and degrade any people who seek to uphold it. War will inevitably follow as the result of an attempt to perpetrate it ... Naked, hideous and revolting, it looms up before us as a monster from the cruel and shameless world which all had hoped and prayed was forever behind us.'[1]

The protestations from the Senate were the first signs of resistance in Washington to both Shandong and the Treaty of Versailles in general. It would end, many months later, with an ailing Wilson unable to ratify the Treaty in his own country, and see the League of Nations doomed to proceed without American participation.

Meanwhile, with pro-American feeling in China at an all-time low and pro-Japanese sympathisers hounded out of government, the immediate winner was Soviet Russia, which answered the American betrayal with a propaganda triumph.

> **If the Chinese nation desires to ... escape the destiny prescribed for it at Versailles ... it should understand that its only allies and brothers in the struggle for liberty are the Russian worker and peasant and the Red Army of Russia.**
>
> **LEV KARAKHAN**

Lev Karakhan, the USSR's Deputy People's Commissar for Foreign Affairs, issued a declaration to China on 25 July 1919. In it, the Soviet Union delivered a promise that had eluded the Great Powers, unilaterally renouncing the unequal treaties in China. The declaration came charged with political insinuations: 'If the Chinese nation desires to become free like the Russian people, and to escape the destiny prescribed for it at Versailles in order to transform it into a second Korea or a second India, it should understand that its only allies and brothers in the struggle for liberty are the Russian worker and peasant and the Red Army of Russia.'[2]

The Karakhan Manifesto, coupled with continuing Japanese aggression in northern China and the popular fervour of the 4 May demonstrations, created a fertile ground for a movement that was neither imperialist, pro-Western, nor pro-Japanese. The USSR was quick to act, setting up the Comintern organisation to foster Soviet ideology in foreign countries. Within a year, China had gained a Socialist Youth League, and a Communist faction was growing within Sun Yatsen's southern government. It encouraged many of the disaffected people of China to switch their allegiance to the only nation that was seen to be sweeping away the traditions of old and looking to the future. It helped nurture the earliest days of the Communist movement in China, which would ultimately seize power from both north and south.

Even with the Treaty of Versailles complete, pressure about Shandong continued from the Great Powers. Britain's Lord Curzon pointedly called on the Japanese Ambassador Chinda Sutemi back in London to ask him when Japan was planning on restoring Shandong to China, as per its assurances at the Conference. Chinda offered vague excuses about the settlement, which fooled nobody. Questions were asked about Shandong in the House of Commons. Back in Paris, where many delegates were still clearing paperwork, Makino Nobuaki faced an American threat to publish Japan's assurances, and a recommendation that Japan would save face if it published them herself. Japan, however, refused, and was widely suspected to be ignoring the rulings of the Peace Conference, in favour of the old 1915 secret treaty. Wilson lost his patience in August, and threatened 'grave embarrassments' unless Japan obliged him with 'immediate assurance'. Japan, however, called Wilson's bluff. Since Wilson's own government was not even prepared to support him on the matter of the Treaty of Versailles, the Japanese did not bother to do so, either.[3]

Politics was not the only concern for Koo at Paris. In the brief period of international approbation following his trouncing of the Japanese in February, and before the unrest and disappointment that met the Shandong decision later in the year, Koo had attracted the attention of a wealthy family of overseas Chinese. His status as a widower with two infant children was well known in the Chinese world, as was his immense eligibility as a prominent Chinese diplomat. This combination proved irresistible to the family of Oei Hui-lan, the privileged daughter of the 'sugar king of Malaysia', who saw to it that Koo received a photograph of her.

Who approached whom is unclear – much of the negotiations were done behind the scenes, and Oei's own autobiography implies that Koo both 'fell in love' with her photograph, but that her own mother and sister veritably pushed her into meeting him. Regardless, as the Conference began to wind down, Koo and Miss Oei were carefully seated next to each other at a banquet, and then made to share a limousine afterwards.

On days when, even in Oei's view, Koo should have been conducting 'his important work as second Chinese delegate to the Peace Conference', he pursued the young debutante with a vengeance, showering her with orchids and other gifts, and officially proposing marriage after only a couple of weeks. There is a rushed, faintly ghoulish quality about the speed of their engagement – Koo's former parents-in-law were both present in Paris at the time, still mourning their daughter, but also complicit in the efforts to steer Oei into accepting Koo's proposal. So, too, was C T Wang, who seemed to have briefly overcome his antipathy for Koo, forgotten his former claims that Koo was about to marry Cao Rulin's daughter, and instead 'employed his famous oratorical powers to praise Wellington Koo in glowing terms'.[4]

The couple announced their engagement on 10 October, at a lavish ball attended by 'almost every nationality', thanks to the stragglers at the Peace Conference, finalising paperwork and deals long after the fateful day at the Hall of Mirrors.

However, they appear to have only told the Chinese in Paris – many of the other foreign guests assumed that Oei, a Kashmir sapphire engagement ring on her finger, was already married to Koo, and indeed that she was the late May Tang, whose death does not appear to have been widely discussed before-hand outside the Chinese circle.

Soon afterwards, Lu Zhengxiang left Paris and returned to China. At Shanghai, 'as I came off the boat, and at all the stations at which my train stopped, great popular demonstra-tions, cheering him who had refused to sign, testified ... that I had interpreted with perception the views of the country, which declared itself to be entirely with me'.[5]

Although Lu was welcomed as the hero of the hour, he owed much of his victory to Wellington Koo, who remained in the West.

Wellington Koo and Oei Hui-lan were married in Brussels at a relatively low-key ceremony at the Chinese Legation on the morning of 14 November 1920.[6] The only relative present was Oei's mother – other ceremonial functions were fulfilled by the Chinese ministers to Belgium and Spain, with their wives as maids of honour. The ceremony was performed by the Chinese military attaché from Paris – since it took place on nominally Chinese soil, Madame Koo would cling in later life to the somewhat extraterritorial notion that she was Koo's 'true' (i.e. Chinese) wife.

For reasons never quite explained, Koo had neglected to mention to several participants, including his young bride, that the official opening of the Assembly of the League of Nations was due to take place the following day. The couple therefore spent the afternoon packing, returned to the Lega-tion for a farewell dinner in their honour, and passed their wedding night on the sleeper train to Geneva, whereupon

Koo was whisked away by his secretaries to prepare for the League's inaugural session.

Back in London, Koo's appointment as a Chinese minister to Great Britain was met with a baffling response from *Punch* magazine. In a misjudged attempt at humour, *Punch* offered a pointless eight-verse ballad in the style of *The Mikado*, which both 'welcomed' Koo to Britain but implied he was nothing more than a mandarin with a funny name.

'Morality, heavenly link,'
I'm sure you will never taboo,
Though to it I don't think you'll 'eternally drink'
Temperate Wellington Koo.

It is rather malicious, I own
To play with a name that is true,
But I hope you'll condone my irreverent tone
Generous Wellington Koo.[7]

Madame Koo reported that Baron Hayashi, the Japanese ambassador to London, used to pay her similarly backhanded compliments that she found infuriating.

'"You know your husband is not really appreciated," he remarked with irritating frequency. 'He is at least twenty years ahead of the present times in China."'[8]

Koo briefly became the Chinese Minister to the Court of Saint James, based at a legation in London's Portland Place. He and his young wife were thrown in at the deep end of London society with a ball at Buckingham Palace, given in honour of the King and Queen of Belgium. Before long, however, Koo was called to Washington in October 1921 to represent Chinese interests at a new peace conference. The new US President, Warren Harding, had run against Wilson on a ticket that included justice for Shandong, which he hoped to arrange at the Conference for the Limitation of Armaments.

It was, according to most versions of the story, in Washington that the most famous anecdote about Wellington Koo came about – it has achieved such notoriety that it even has its own page on the Internet, although Madame Koo cast doubts upon its veracity in her memoirs. Supposedly, Koo was a guest at a lavish hotel dinner for the diplomatic community. Unaware of the identity of the Chinese gentleman at his table, an American diner tried to think of something to say to the strange foreigner. Eventually, as the first course was coming to a close, he addressed Koo with a patronising tone, asking: 'You likee soupee-soupee?'

Koo nodded diplomatically, and said nothing else. However, he was soon called up to the podium to deliver the keynote address, whereupon he regaled the crowd with a speech on international affairs, conducted in fluent English. As he finished his speech, he sat down to rapturous applause, turned to his neighbour and asked in a loud voice: *You likee speechee-speechee?*

Koo's main ally in Washington was China's local representative, his old Paris associate Alfred Sze, but he was up against a list of heavyweight Japanese delegates, including the Japanese navy minister Kato Tomosaburō, the ambassador to the US Shidehara Kijurō, and Tokugawa Iesato, the adopted son of the last Shōgun. Controversially for the Japanese, Tokugawa agreed to many American suggestions on arms limitations, but as far as the Chinese were concerned, the issue of Shandong was of far greater importance.

Koo and his assistants ensured that the arguments dragged on, since instead of targeting specific details, they first insisted on establishing basic principles of justice on which all delegates could agree. In November Koo presented the Conference with his Ten Points, a document which aimed at preventing any foreign power from willingly entering into a situation which might cause a future question to arise like that of Shandong. China's right as a neutral state was to be 'fully respected' in future by belligerents, and other clauses broadly abolished special rights and privileges for foreigners in China, including extraterritoriality. Foreign powers were also to agree 'not to conclude between themselves any treaty or agreement directly affecting China or the general peace.' The Ten Points were later incorporated in the four-part Root Resolution adopted by the Conference in December 1921, which softened much of the language, but still agreed to 'respect the territorial integrity of China.' This resulted in the Nine Power Treaty of 1922, 'a policy to stabilise conditions in the Far East' that would form the groundwork of subsequent debate at the League of Nations in the ensuing 15 years.[9]

Koo gained a degree of success in pursuing China's right to trade tariff autonomy. This discussion, however, was rendered toothless by the concept that it would not come entirely into force until it had been signed by every nation with a trade agreement with China, including non-signatory powers that were not represented at the Conference.

The big issue for the Chinese, however, remained the issue that had caused them to abstain from signing the Treaty – the Shandong Question. Despite Warren Harding's bold claims for Shandong during his election campaign, it was left off the initial agenda of the Washington Conference. The Versailles decision returned to haunt the Chinese at Washington, with America reluctant to include it in general discussions as

Britain, France and Italy had already approved the terms of Versailles, and hence would not take kindly to the terms being altered after their assent.

Of greater use to the Chinese was another promise left over from the Peace Conference – the assurance by the Japanese that they would *eventually* restore Shandong. This presented an ideal loophole, since the delegates need not debate the *hows* and *whys*, but instead get straight to the *whens*. Shidehara offered proposed terms of a settlement in September 1921, which attempted to leave the railway and police force in 'joint' Sino-Japanese hands. This, as Koo had already observed in Paris, handed over *the shadow but not the substance*, as the railway and its guardians would enjoy *de facto* control of the entire peninsula. The Americans agreed, noting that Japan had agreed to *restore* control to China, and not to keep half of everything for itself.

Frustrated with the lack of progress, Koo went for a drive in the country with his pregnant wife, only to return to find the entrance hall of his rented house crowded with irate Chinese students, who were sure that he was about to sell out on Shandong. 'They had pushed the servants aside,' wrote Madame Koo, 'and cut the telephone wires, insistent on some kind of foolish violence.' [10]

Koo successfully talked the intruders out of doing anyone any harm, answering their queries, and occupying them until the arrival of the police dispelled the trouble. The students were opposed to any form of direct negotiation between China and Japan, because it would not only tacitly agree to the Twenty-One Demands, but would also acknowledge the terms of the Treaty of Versailles.

By December, the Chinese and the Japanese were at the table to discuss the railway, with the Japanese still pushing for a 'joint' arrangement. Koo, no stranger to the world of arranged marriages, likened the Japanese request to a doomed wedding, which would never succeed for as long as one of the participants was acting under duress. Instead, in something of a compromise, Koo offered for China to buy the Japanese half of the railway, thereby ensuring that Japan was not out of pocket. This might have seemed reasonable on paper, and the Paris Peace Conference had already agreed a value for the railway. However, the accounting soon became much messier, with the agreed value of the railway as the Japanese had found it, subject to the debatable value of improvements made to the railway by the Japanese during the period they had assumed Shandong would belong to them. Shidehara denied that China could even claim to be the legal owner of the railway, merely of the ground over which the substance of the railway was built – one gets a sense, in the Washington debates, of Shakespeare's Shylock and his pound of flesh.

As Christmas loomed, Shidehara offered a complicated 20-year lend-lease agreement on the railway, from which China could buy itself out after ten years if it could come up with the money. The plan seemed good, but faltered over the discussion of guarantors and safeguards, with Koo noting that if the Japanese were demanding third-party monitors (which they were), it implied that they didn't trust the Chinese, which was hardly a good beginning to a bilateral international agreement.[11]

Koo stated openly that his interest was in clearing the Japanese out of Shandong as swiftly as possible, in order to avoid further 'misunderstandings'. He favoured a swift payment in only a few years, whereas the Japanese pushed for a much longer period of perhaps 40 years – their argument being that railways took time to earn back the cost of their construction.

Koo, however, was swift to note that the Japanese claims over what was 'normal' applied to railways before they were built. The railway across Shandong was already in existence, so would not require quite the same amount of time to amass its profits.

There was much more wrangling along similar lines, ending with the Japanese delegates agreeing to recommend a 12-year repayment, and an effective power of Chinese veto over the appointment of Japanese officials. It was a wearying and, as the reader may agree, dull process of argument and counter-argument, and sadly meant very little, considering Japan's subsequent invasion of China in the 1930s.

Without Koo's knowledge, the Japanese were trying precisely the kind of arm-twisting behind the scenes that he had expected. Even as Koo and Shidehara were politely debating Shandong in Washington, the Japanese minister in Beijing, Obata Torikichi, was calling on the Chinese head of state, threatening to have the negotiations aborted, and making the somewhat ironic claim that Japanese ministers were in no position to make promises on behalf of the Japanese government – in Obata's case, it would seem that ministers had no trouble making threats on the same basis. The news came out through the southern Chinese government of Sun Yatsen, which stirred things up by cabling Washington to reveal the details of the Obata meeting, and noting that Koo and his associates might want to check with Beijing before rejecting offers of much-needed Japanese money.

The cable was misleading, but caused immense trouble both for Koo, who faced more crowds of angry Chinese demonstrators, and for Beijing, which suddenly faced troop movements from angry warlords in six provinces, who threatened to secede from the Chinese Republic. Barely two weeks into 1922, the Chinese Premier had been forced to resign, and the position of Koo and his delegates had been compromised. Koo made one final offer to the Japanese, but noted that the Chinese people did not want to be in hock once more to Japanese loans that they did not really need. He also suggested, as subtly as he could, that it might be wise to bring in Britain (Arthur Balfour) and America (Charles Evans Hughes) to 'help' at the final negotiations, in case they had any fresh ideas or input that might aid a final decision. It was a diplomatic way of reprimanding everyone who had doubted him – just as he had predicted, it was impossible for Japan to negotiate with China unsupervised, as it only resulted in underhand tactics.

The final settlement, brokered with the aid of Hughes and Balfour, offered a 15-year payment by the Chinese, redeemable at any time after five years, and what amounted to joint control by Sino-Japanese appointees. Balfour warned Koo that this was the best anyone could do – Japan already had control of the Shandong railway, and short of a new war, it seemed that there was no other way to get the Japanese to budge. The Chinese government, or what was left of it, agreed to the idea, and authorised Koo to sign, after literally months of negotiations.

Nor was the handover of Shandong going to be as easy. The Germans had, it transpired, burned all the deeds and titles to land in Qingdao during their retreat, which would mean disentangling land ownership in the area was going to be troublesome. Despite the absence of many documents, the Japanese immediately asked for certain public buildings – including cemeteries and shrines – to be left in the care of 'the Japanese community'. An exasperated Koo commented that he was not in a position to judge from Washington whether the buildings had been built by the Japanese, and thought it best that such details were left to others.

The Koo entourage returned to Europe, after disposing of several cases of leftover wine among their friends and colleagues. America was still under Prohibition at the time, but the Chinese had arrived with ample supplies of European alcohol, smuggled in under the cloak of diplomatic immunity.[12]

Wellington Koo (far right) at an informal meeting of the United Nations' 'Big Four' at the Fairmont Hotel in San Francisco in 1945. The others (left to right) are Lord Halifax (Great Britain), Secretary of State Edward Stettinius (USA), and A A Gromyko (USSR).

III

The Legacy

8
China in Chaos

Despite, or rather because of his successes abroad, Koo was recalled to China in 1922, where he received a hero's welcome. He was called to serve as a minister for Foreign Affairs in an administration that was determined to use 'Able Men' to further China's interests. Koo's fame at the time was such that a poll in a local English-language newspaper ranked him as the third greatest living Chinese. But his appointment was made out of desperation – China was almost bankrupt and faced economic collapse within six months. It was hoped that Koo, who had scored such glorious victories in Paris and Washington, would be able to surpass himself by negotiating China out of penury. In particular, it was hoped that he could put a stop to the remaining Boxer Indemnities, and secure much-needed foreign loans.

Koo's contacts in the US and Britain stood him in good stead, but Japan observed that China was already defaulting on previous agreements, and that further delays and suspensions would only throw good money after bad. The 'Able Men' government was soon out of office, and the next six years found a revolving door of appointments and cabinets.

Koo was only recalled as Foreign Minister when China found itself in another impossible mess, which seemed tailor-made to unravel many of Koo's diplomatic achievements. On 5 May 1923, a group of bandits ambushed a northbound train in Lincheng on its way to Tianjin. The bandits saw themselves as soldiers, part of a 6,000-strong group feuding with a rival warlord coalition further to the north. They kidnapped some 200 passengers and dragged them to a notoriously well-defended mountain stronghold. The Lincheng Incident was a sad sign of the breakdown of Chinese society, as rival warlords jostled for supremacy, but the incident might have passed were it not for the passengers on the train. Although most of the hostages were Chinese, the bandits had managed to acquire 19 foreigners, including 16 Americans, one of whom was the editor of a Shanghai newspaper. A British subject was killed in the attack, but there were soon stories circulating that although there had been Japanese passengers on the train, none of them were taken hostage. Furthermore, it was alleged that the bandits had three Japanese military advisers in their camp, and one of their demands was that a notoriously pro-Japanese general should be appointed governor of Shandong.

Koo was recalled to run damage-control, but did so while unwilling to associate himself directly with the administration. In a public statement, he announced he was *taking office because the majority of the members of the Parliament have urged him to do so, and because he deemed it his duty to undertake upholding China's international position.*[1]

Koo faced foreign demands for reparations that compared Lincheng to a new Boxer Rebellion. Using tactics he had previously employed in Paris, Koo leaked details of the demands to the press, revealing that in spite of the smiling assurances made at the Washington Conference, foreign powers were demanding their own troops in China to protect their own interests, and had even suggested that China might require an 'international regency'. Koo maintained a stern position, pointing out that it was counterproductive and misleading to compare what was essentially a train robbery to the Boxer Rebellion, which had been an anti-foreign crusade.

Koo was not part of the negotiations with the bandits, which ended in June with the offering of a government pardon, the exchange of pleasantries, and the integration of the kidnappers into the Chinese army. All the hostages were released, although once the brigands were out of the mountains, still wearing their newly provided Chinese military uniforms, they were ambushed, their leader shot, and the forces disbanded.

The Lincheng Incident, largely forgotten today amid the reversals of the following decade, led to calls in the international community for the return of foreign troops to China. The result was as if an international vote of no confidence had been proclaimed in China's ability to run its own affairs. Amid accusations that the railway staff had been in league with the bandits, there were calls for foreign controls on China's railway. In a measured response, Koo reiterated that Lincheng was … *not a case of anti-foreign demonstration, nor did it betray a symptom of special animosity against foreigners as such. It arose simply from an act of lawlessness committed by Brigands … . Careful consideration of the case leads to the conclusion that no liability for damages can be predicated of the Chinese government.*[2]

Although the incident was embarrassing for China, and few outside China believed Koo's assurances that the government was still in control, Koo's intercession and diplomacy may have averted a foreign troop deployment that would have rivalled that of the Boxer Rebellion.

Koo noted that he hoped he had *cleared up the false impression which has been current that China is in a state of not being governed.*[3] Ironically, however, Koo was in far more danger in his home country than he had ever been as a foreign diplomat. His antipathy towards Japan was well known, and pro-Japanese newspapers wasted no time in manufacturing scandal. When Madame Koo, exasperated at the number of banquets at the Koo residence, demanded that Koo entertain his political cronies elsewhere, the Japanese press soon ran with the headline: 'Madame Koo versus Koo Cabinet!'

Not all attacks were mere paper dragons. In summer 1923, Wellington and his once-more pregnant wife came down with a violent bout of what first appeared to be food poisoning. Several of their servants disappeared never to be seen again, and analysis of their dinner the previous night showed traces of arsenic.

The period also saw Koo caught between rising pro-Communist feeling in China, and under heavy pressure to recognise the Soviet Union. Koo's native Shanghai had become home to thousands of White Russian refugees, a fact which is likely to have coloured his unwillingness to recognise the overtures of the USSR for recognition. Moreover, the Soviets were also dealing directly with the southern Chinese government in Canton, leading to the very real possibility that Koo's northern regime might find itself trapped once more between opponents. In February 1924, Britain and Italy officially recognised the Soviet Union as the legitimate government of Russia, placing Koo under even heavier pressure, particularly in Outer Mongolia, which had utilised Soviet aid in resisting a Chinese attempt to retake control in 1919.

The Karakhan Manifesto had gained powerful support for the new USSR in China, as had the Soviet cancellation of Russia's entitlement to its Boxer Indemnity. However, the Soviet Union insisted on independence for Outer Mongolia, which many in the Chinese administration still regarded as part of China – it had been conceded by Yuan Shikai, but not every Chinese official had recognised the Yuan government that had conceded it. Furthermore, the United States still refused to recognise the Soviet Union as the legitimate government of Russia, and Koo was keen to follow the American lead. Koo's eternal rival C T Wang prepared a document outlining agreements between China and the USSR. At first glance, it seemed excellent, normalising relations with the Soviet Union and cancelling all China's treaties with the USSR's Tsarist predecessor. However, it pointedly did *not* cancel a 1921 treaty between the USSR and the Mongolian People's Republic, which was currently occupied by Soviet troops. Koo realised that this was because the Soviets did not recognise Mongolia as part of China – if he were to agree to the Wang-Karakhan document, he would sign away Mongolia forever. Nor was Koo happy with a demand from the atheist Soviet state that Russian Orthodox missionary property in China now belonged to the USSR. For Koo, this set a dangerous precedent for the transferral of missions all over China into the hands of belligerent powers. This in turn could lead to multiple conflicts over jurisdiction, sovereignty and, yes, extraterritoriality – in the wrong hands, this simple clause might be the basis of an entire new generation of Unequal Treaties.[4]

C T Wang was angry – if sent back to re-open negotiations, he would lose face with both the Soviets and the Chinese. Koo was obliged to tell Karakhan himself that Wang had not been authorised to conclude negotiations, leading to an escalating diplomatic stand-off that found the Soviets in secret talks with the Japanese, and Chinese ministers in Moscow frozen out of diplomatic events. Koo became subject to the same kind of popular pressure that had dogged his time in Paris, facing ardent student protests that demanded China accept the proposals of what many intellectuals believed to be a benign Soviet ally.

Regardless of public opinion to the contrary, Koo had good reason to mistrust the motives of foreign powers. On 15 May 1924, a sumptuously wrapped package arrived at his Beijing house, post-marked from the hometown of the incumbent president. Opened by a group of the Koo servants, who had gathered round with typical Chinese curiosity to inspect the contents and divide up the golden seals on the outside, the package exploded, killing one and badly injuring two others. The sender was apprehended but escaped, tellingly, to Japan, before he could reveal his motives or superiors.[5]

Koo reluctantly signed an agreement with Karakhan later in the month, effectively giving up on Outer Mongolia, which became a Soviet satellite state. Relations between China and the USSR were, at least, returned to normal, keeping the countries from war, but also opening China to further incursions by Comintern agents. While the Soviets continued to plot with the southern Chinese government in Canton, the USSR stopped short of recognising the Canton administration, and instead recognised Beijing's. Meanwhile, C T Wang himself dispelled Koo's concerns about the Orthodox missions, pointing out that in order for the USSR to gain those concessions, it had first renounced all Unequal Treaties and trade tariffs with China, including any claim on the Boxer Indemnity. As far as Wang was concerned, any country was welcome to the same deal if it would reciprocate with a similar offer, and for the price of a few scraps of real estate, China could accomplish what decades of diplomacy had failed to achieve.[6]

Koo also attempted to restart negotiations with the British over Weihaiwei, the prime seaport on the eastern tip of Shandong, which had originally been leased for 25 years from 1898. Later agreements had established that the British would keep Weihaiwei for as long as the Japanese were in Port Arthur, but Koo hoped to establish that such agreements had been made under duress, and that it would be in British interests to hand Weihaiwei back on the original agreed date, which had already passed. Negotiations broke down with the outbreak of a coup in Beijing in 1924 that was soon trumped by the arrival of a nearby warlord's army. Koo was forced to flee the city, ironically to Weihaiwei, where the British presence he had tried to oust probably saved his life.[7]

Another refugee from the attack on Beijing was the former Last Emperor, Puyi, who was spirited out of his father's house by his tutor Reginald Johnston, and taken to the Legation quarter. Johnston and Puyi eluded his minders and went in search of a Legation where Puyi could claim asylum. Ironically, the first ambassador they found was the British Ronald Macleay, who had offered such memorably minimal support to the Chinese at the Paris Peace Conference. Macleay informed Johnston that 'It has never been the practice of this Legation to receive political refugees.' In desperation, Johnston sent Puyi to the Japanese Legation, where he was welcomed and eventually smuggled out of town to safety. The Last Emperor thereby made his way into Japanese hands, with dire consequences for China in the ensuing decade.[8]

Beijing was 'rescued' a month later when yet another warlord ousted the previous occupant. Although still nominally the seat of a democratic China, the city was now entirely under the sway of the 'Old Marshal' Zhang Zuolin, the warlord of Manchuria. A former bandit, Zhang had risen to legitimate military prominence fighting on the Russian side against the Japanese in the Russo-Japanese War of 1904–5. With the fall of imperial China, Zhang had been made military governor of Mukden under the administration of Yuan Shikai, an authority soon extended to all of Manchuria. By seizing Beijing, Zhang was now the only candidate for head of state of what was left of the northern government. Zhang was no elected official, but unlike China's southern government, he refused to consider an alliance with the Soviets, and favoured the gradual advance of China's diplomatic position – this alone made Wellington Koo prepared to deal with him. Zhang's reign in Beijing, however, bore disturbing echoes of the trappings of empire. On his first day as the new dictator, he travelled to the Temple of Confucius in a large procession, walking on a pathway of yellow sand, an imperial affectation.[9]

Sun Yatsen travelled to Beijing in an attempt to broker a peace deal between the rival governments, but he was already seriously ill from cancer, and died at Koo's house. Sun was succeeded in the south by Chiang Kai-shek, who initially favoured a Soviet alliance, placing him at odds with the north. In 1926, Chiang launched the Northern Expedition, a military campaign to unite north and south by force.

With willing politicians in such short supply, Zhang's cabinet were obliged to share posts, and Koo, returning from his brief exile, briefly served as both the Chinese Prime Minister and Foreign Minister. His tenure coincided with the decision by Britain to withdraw its recognition of the Beijing regime. The rise of Zhang Zuolin had been the final straw, and although Britain held off on recognising Chiang Kai-shek immediately, it hoped to broker an international memorandum to the effect that Chiang Kai-shek's southern government enjoyed a greater claim to be the government of China.

The British ambassador, Miles Lampson, came to discuss this with Koo, who snootily asked to see his credentials. When Lampson replied that he would provide his papers when his superiors recognised Koo's government, Koo brought up the Nine Power Treaty that had been agreed in Washington. Under the Washington terms, foreign powers had to consult China before taking such decisions regarding its internal politics. Far from acceding to Lampson's demands, Zhang Zuolin was rather hoping for increased British assistance against what he saw as the Communist sympathisers in the southern government. Britain, however, continued to favour the southern regime, and in December 1926, Sir Francis Aglen, the British Inspector-General of the Chinese Maritime Customs Administration went south for an ominous meeting.

Aglen's favour was crucial to the survival of a Chinese government. The customs revenue he oversaw represented 30 per cent of Beijing's state income, and if he were to switch allegiances to the south, it would spell the end of the northern Chinese regime. Zhang's government hoped to gain a loan secured on the customs revenue that had once been the Austro-Hungarian Boxer Indemnity. Aglen was recalled from leave in England but deliberately dawdled, awarding himself a month's sojourn in south-east Asia on the way home, and upon his tardy arrival in Beijing, refused to agree to the deal. Aglen's behaviour was raised at a Cabinet meeting, met with unanimous disapproval, and resulted in Koo's decision to sack him for insubordination.

The incident was a great shock to the Chinese banking community, to whom Aglen had functioned as an unofficial, unelected finance minister, and led to a strong protest from the British ambassador, and dire warnings from the Americans. Koo, however, held firm, and the incident soon blew over, leading him to observe that *if China stood on her legitimate rights, her action, no matter how striking or even shocking it might appear in the Far East or Asia in general, would be fully understood abroad.*[10]

Koo continued to dismantle the Unequal Treaties. When Belgium's treaty with China ran out without being renegotiated, Koo simply proclaimed it as null and void. He then used the Belgian precedent to get a better deal with Spain, and announced to the Japanese and French that they were next on his list. He achieved such 'successes', in part, because few took the regime he represented seriously any more. Chiang Kai-shek's expedition drew ever nearer and the Old Marshal, despite having a powerful modern army, did not place enough trust in his subordinates to send them southwards to fight. Only confident on his home ground in Manchuria, the Old Marshal withdrew, and made overtures to Chiang to the effect that there was no need for them to fight. Manchuria was his, the rest of China was Chiang's, and with that in mind, perhaps they should just shake hands and declare China unified.

> **If China stood on her legitimate rights, her action, no matter how striking or even shocking it might appear in the Far East or Asia in general, would be fully understood abroad.**
> **WELLINGTON KOO**

Koo's tenure as Prime Minister was ended in June 1927 with the arrival of Chiang Kai-shek's troops in Beijing. Koo resigned and went into retirement, leaving Beijing in the hands of Chiang's party, the Guomindang. Chiang's 'unified' China was still riven with warlordism. The Old Marshal's deal allowed him to keep Manchuria, but north and south China were, at least on paper, now a single entity. Koo, however, was regarded as a flunky of the northern regime, and was distinctly unpopular with many members of the new government, including his old Paris adversary C T Wang.

Koo fled once again for Weihaiwei under an assumed name, ahead of a warrant for his own arrest. There, he sought asylum with the British, whose commissioner, Reginald Johnston, former tutor to the Last Emperor, observed: 'Although Dr Koo is one of the Chinese statesmen who had advocated the abolition of the "Unequal Treaties", and foreign concessions, he has on several occasions shown himself very ready to avail himself of the protection which those treaties and concessions afforded to ... embarrassed Chinese politicians to find peace and protection here under the British flag.' [11]

Koo spent the next 18 months in exile, at least officially on a 'fishing trip' in France and Canada. During his absence, Chiang Kai-shek's government was officially recognised by the United States. Britain favoured Chiang Kai-shek with the restoration of tariff autonomy, and Weihaiwei, the Shandong harbour that had offered Koo sanctuary, was reverted to the Chinese. To a certain extent, much of Koo's foreign diplomacy came to fruition. However, within China itself, there was still chaos among rival factions and intrigues by the Japanese.

The most notable of these came in 1928, and, predictably, involved a railway. Officers of the Japanese army, who were supposedly in Manchuria to protect Japan's rail interests, instead used their position to plant a bomb on a bridge over the very railway they were supposed to be guarding. As Zhang Zuolin's train was passing under the bridge the Japanese soldiers set off the bomb, killing several of Zhang's officials. Zhang himself died several hours later.

It had been hoped by the Japanese that Zhang's son Xue-liang, 'the Young Marshal' would be easier to manipulate. Still in his twenties, the Young Marshal was addicted to opium and, it was thought, open to Japanese strong-arm tactics. In fact, the assassination of his father turned the Young Marshal against any thought of Japanese collaboration. He purged Japanese influences from his inner circle, and began to favour a rapprochement with Chiang Kai-shek's Nationalist government. Thanks to the Young Marshal's powerful position in Manchuria, and his influence on the new rulers of China, Wellington Koo would soon be able to revive a diplomatic career that would have otherwise been in tatters.

9
The Spreading Whirlpool

In 1929, Koo returned to China, positive that his service to a now-discredited regime was sure to disqualify him from holding any future offices in the Chinese government. *I wanted to leave the political sphere*, he recounted, *and had the intention of giving up my political and diplomatic life altogether. But things do not always turn out as one might wish.*[1] Koo's decision to seek an alternate career was inspired in part by the hostility felt towards him by his rivals in the Nanjing government, particularly C T Wang. Instead, he went to Manchuria, where the warlord Zhang Xueliang, nominally now an ally of Chiang Kai-shek, offered him sanctuary. Zhang Xueliang was the ruler of all territory north of the Great Wall, and his foreign adviser, William Donald, was an old acquaintance of Koo's from Beijing in the days of Yuan Shikai. Koo and the Young Marshal played golf together and discussed foreign policy, while Zhang sternly requested that his allies in the Nanjing government rescind their order for Koo's arrest. Nanjing needed the warlord's help in dealing with another breakaway regime, this time in the far south in Guangzhou (Canton), and that gave the Young Marshal extra leverage. However, the Young Marshal's main concerns were in his own domain, which remained under the threat of Japanese interference. Chiang Kai-shek, unhelpfully, warned his new ally not to attempt any actions in Manchuria that would provoke the Japanese into a retaliation that might so easily transform into the acquisition of more territory.

Koo had warned the Young Marshal of the likelihood of Japanese activity in Manchuria, but Zhang had thrown his memo in a drawer. Now that it had come true with the Japanese terrorist attack, a shaken Zhang called Koo to his side for advice. Koo advocated an immediate appeal to the League of Nations. Zhang wired to Chiang Kai-shek's Nanjing government for military assistance, but none was forthcoming. Instead, Chiang was off on another campaign in the hinterland against the Communists, who he now regarded as a greater threat to China's security than the Japanese. Perhaps realising that only one man stood a chance of steering China through League of Nations scrutiny, Chiang telegraphed Koo with the offer of a position in his administration, as Minister of Foreign Affairs. Still smarting from two years of exile under Chiang's arrest order, it was Koo's turn to refuse.

> I wanted to leave the political sphere and had the intention of giving up my political and diplomatic life altogether. But things do not always turn out as one might wish.
>
> **WELLINGTON KOO**

Chiang's incumbent Foreign Minister was still Koo's old nemesis C T Wang. At the time that Koo was being offered his job, Wang was at the Nanjing foreign office, under attack from a mob of angry Chinese students, who beat him badly and left him for dead. Riots had broken out in Shanghai and Nanjing over the Japanese invasion and over the Chinese government's apparent lack of response. Amid increasingly stern cables from Nanjing, Wang was smuggled onto a gunboat to Shanghai to recuperate.

In 1930, Koo was in Shanghai himself, attending the funeral of his mother – presumably secure in the knowledge that the Guomindang no longer wanted him in custody. The Guomindang in Nanjing took the opportunity to invite him again to take up a government post, claiming that all was forgiven. Koo relented and took his rival's post, in the government that had only recently tried to have him arrested.

In 1931, the Japanese made their move against Manchuria, in what would later be known as the Mukden Incident. A small amount of explosives went off near a section of the South Manchurian Railway, causing so little damage to the tracks that the next train to pass was able to do so with only the slightest discernible wobble – the area of affected railway was later assessed at just 31 inches. This, however, was reported further afield as a terrible terrorist incident perpetrated by the Chinese, against which the Japanese were now obliged to take military action. Within two days, Japanese reinforcements had arrived across the border from Korea, and the Japanese had occupied Mukden (Shenyang), the capital of Manchuria. Zhang Xueliang's soldiers, under orders from Chiang Kai-shek not to resist Japanese aggression, either fled or surrendered. The action was reported in Japan as an incredible victory for the young officers in charge, even though they had provoked the incident themselves without the approval of their superiors.

Chiang Kai-shek announced that the incident would be settled by the League of Nations, a proclamation of remarkable, albeit misguided, faith in the efficacy of that organisation. Koo did not share his faith in the League, since he now expected little more than a repeat of the solemn, unfulfilled promises and Japanese brinkmanship of the Paris Peace Conference. For his part, Koo served as Foreign Minister in Nanjing for three overworked months, quartered, with inadvertent irony, in the Ministry of Railways, heavily guarded and forced to travel by armoured car. Meanwhile, student protestors called for China to walk out of the League of Nations, at one point surrounding the Foreign Ministry and pursuing Koo down the street, so that he had to take refuge in Chiang Kai-shek's house. Chinese diplomats were not even safe abroad – in Geneva, Alfred Sze was attacked by Chinese students and subsequently resigned his position on the League Council.

In Geneva, Japanese representatives pressed for the Manchurian matter to be settled between China and Japan without League interference – the very sort of exclusion that had ruined China's chances of achieving a reasonable settlement over the Twenty-One Demands. Remembering the far better results he had achieved at the Washington Peace Conference, Koo urged Chiang to enter into direct negotiations with the Japanese, under the aegis of a powerful third party such as the United States.

The Japanese continued to milk the diplomatic system, demanding that Chiang first recognise Japanese treaty rights in Manchuria before entering into further negotiations. To its credit, the League Council voted against the Japanese proposals, and instead agreed with China that the Japanese should first pull back their troops. But even as the Japanese delegates argued over the points in Geneva, the army they supposedly controlled was continuing to advance across Chinese territory.

No stranger to Japanese manipulation of the customs of

diplomacy, Koo saw the League negotiations for what they were, an extended delaying tactic. The decision to send a League Commission to investigate in Manchuria, Koo told the American minister in Nanjing, was *vague in its terms, it provided no time limit for evacuation, and it provided no method of bringing China and Japan together for a general settlement of outstanding questions.*[2] Instead, Koo suggested it would be far more sensible for the Japanese to withdraw from the territory they had so swiftly occupied, and await the outcome of a multinational conference on the incident. Koo argued that even talking about a League investigation was just a Japanese smokescreen, designed to delay the involvement of the international community for vital weeks while the Japanese consolidated their hold on their new territorial gains. *By the time any Commission reaches Manchuria from Europe,* said an exasperated Koo, *Japan will have been in undisturbed occupation there long enough to encourage the organization of an independent government prepared to recognize the position of Japan in Manchuria.*[3]

Koo was right. Even as he was arguing in Shanghai, the Japanese were in the process of setting up the new state of Manchukuo. The deposed Last Emperor of China, Puyi, who had been in Japanese hands since 1924, was installed as the new ruler of a land encompassing his ancestral homeland: the former Chinese provinces of Manchuria, from the Russian border and the edge of Japanese-occupied Korea down to the Great Wall. Japanese 'advisers' and vice-ministers ran the state behind a front of local politicians. Japan immediately recognised Manchukuo as a legitimate state, although other nations were slow to follow its lead.

This was, thought Koo, the moment to invoke the Nine Power Treaty that he had arranged in Washington a decade earlier. Surely this was precisely the sort of invasion of a sovereign state's territorial integrity that the Nine Power Treaty had been designed to address? While the international community sat on its hands, the Japanese navy arrived off the coast of Shanghai, where it commenced a punitive assault in answer to Chinese sanctions. Koo's latter days as Foreign Minister were spent attempting to broker a cease-fire between the Chinese 19th Route Army and the Japanese aggressors. He did so in council meetings also attended by representatives of the foreign settlements in Shanghai, who soon grew tired with Japanese self-justifications and evasions

At one point in the negotiations, in the midst of yet another Japanese speech, the Australian consultant William Donald asked the British minister Miles Lampson if he knew how pasta-makers put the holes in macaroni. This question, passed in a note among the non-Japanese delegation, soon caused a ripple of heated discussions to break out around the table, resulting in the Italian representative Count Galeazzo Ciano, to send an aide back to his consulate to find out. The Japanese were left entirely baffled by the whispers and gestures around the table, and vexed even more by the respectful silence that greeted the return of Ciano's secretary. With great gravity, Ciano rose to his feet and addressed his fellow negotiators.

'Gentlemen,' he said. 'It is put in by machinery.' [4]

The room erupted in laughter from all except the Japanese, who had not been in on the schoolboy diversion, and believed that some sort of plot was being hatched against them. The presence of so many foreigners in Shanghai, however, helped to bring the case to the international community's notice swifter than actions in Manchuria. The British in Shanghai, unwilling to take unilateral action against Japan, sent a strongly worded request to the League, invoking the Nine Power Treaty as a good reason for a united stand against the aggressor. Eventually, the Japanese attack was brought to a standstill – it was not lost on Koo that the Shanghai Chinese had not withdrawn on this occasion, but had fought to maintain their territory. Since the Japanese were beaten back, standing and fighting seemed to achieve much better effects than vainly waiting for the League to send a rebuke.

Only a few weeks after he left his post, Koo was appointed as China's member on the Lytton Commission, the body tasked with reporting on the Mukden Incident, and in assessing the appropriate response from the League of Nations. The Commission began with a fortnight in Shanghai, and then travelled to Nanjing, and north to Manchuria itself. In almost every city through which the Commission's motorcade drove *en route* to its work, triumphal arches had been erected bearing the Chinese phrase: 'Long Live Wellington Koo.'

> Everyone, peasants, coolies, shopkeepers, even the autocratic northern military commanders shared an almost mystical faith in the power of the League of Nations.
>
> HUI-LAN KOO

'Everyone, peasants, coolies, shopkeepers, even the autocratic northern military commanders,' wrote Madame Koo, 'shared an almost mystical faith in the power of the League of Nations.' [5]

Koo's fellow assessors were a bizarrely mismatched bunch. Lytton himself was an enthusiastic mountaineer, who took the opportunity to scale several Chinese peaks. Henri Claudel, for France, brought a touch of the old Clemenceau charm by displaying what many began to regard as a deliberate, pig-headed contrariness to every suggestion. Despite its uncomfortable absence from the League itself, America had sent its own representative in the form of General Frank Ross McCoy, whose presence only added to Chinese hopes for the Commission's success. Among the other assessors, the Chinese were most irritated by a Mr Yoshida, the Japanese representative, who remained affable and enthusiastic, and 'not the least embarrassed by his awkward role'. One of the few women in the group was the unstoppable Madame Koo, who revelled in her status, and was soon giving 'interviews' to the accompanying newsreel journalists, which were carefully stage-managed by the Young Marshal's aide, William Donald.[6]

The Commission began its travels in Shanghai, but as it neared Manchuria, the Italian ambassador in Japan received a warning, which he duly passed on, that Wellington Koo's life would be in danger if he crossed the border. Koo was troubled enough by the threat to make a will before he entered Manchuria, and slept each night with a peasant disguise by his bed, ready for a quick getaway in case of trouble. Madame Koo, left behind in Beijing, also badgered him into wearing a bespoke bulletproof vest. Koo was not even allowed to go to the bathroom without an escort, and the Commission was rightly convinced that just as their access to Manchuria was being 'managed', so too was the access afforded to interviewees – it was doubtful that the Commission was able to question any Manchurian residents who had not been pre-approved by the Japanese invaders.

Apart from the jolly Mr Yoshida, the Japanese maintained an unofficial presence, with spies in ludicrously conspicuous numbers, who remained mostly harmless, but, in the words of Madame Koo, were 'sprinkled thick as ants over the countryside' and 'maddeningly underfoot'. William

Donald eventually grew so irritated with the two men who were ineptly shadowing him that he grabbed them both in an armlock and frog-marched them to their superior officer with a demand for better-trained agents. Despite the ominous warnings of danger, nobody in the Commission seems to have taken the Japanese spies seriously – the clerks tormented conspicuous lurkers in the hotel lobby by sending them complimentary pots of coffee, and Madame Robert Haas, wife of the secretary-general of the Commission, even called the bluff of a man found ransacking her room. When he claimed to be 'tidying', she facetiously took him at his word, and refused to let him leave until he had scrubbed her floor.

In Mukden itself, Koo was treated to the sight of grim-faced Chinese citizens, forced to assemble for a military parade, ostensibly by the local government of Manchukuo, although Koo noted sourly that only the Japanese seemed to be cheering. On his return to China, he noted at a press conference: *All fellow workers were heart-broken when we witnessed the suffering of our 30 million fellow countrymen and the lost territory, abundant in natural resources. We should look farther, any personal opinion is small and any matter can be sacrificed. But if we fail in diplomacy, we all would perish … . People who came to talk to us usually disappeared the next day.*[7]

Koo was convinced that if Manchukuo were left unchallenged, it would one day form the 'spearhead' of a Japanese invasion of the rest of China. He prepared extensive documents to this effect for the Lytton Commission, and heard that his next appointment, that of Chinese minister to France, would handily put him in Europe – for the first time in ten years, he would be able to attend the League of Nations sessions personally in Geneva, to see the Lytton Commission's report through its next stage. But Koo's faith was not in the League of Nations itself, but in the obligations imposed on some of its members, and indeed the absent United States, by the Nine Power Treaty that had been concluded in Washington. *The League was only an agent of arbitration,* he warned Chiang Kai-shek, *and not an agency of enforcement ... it was a mistake to depend on the League to settle disputes ... we much depend on our own strength to survive in national disaster ... united, we survive and divided, we perish.*[8] Tellingly, Koo had to deliver this information to Chiang Kai-shek at a remote mountain base, where Chiang was still pursuing his vendetta against the Chinese Communists, while Japanese soldiers continued to rampage through Manchuria.

As he left China, Koo promised the press that *he would try his best to struggle for national glory at the League of Nations, and in the meanwhile, hoped that the country would be united to back up the diplomacy.*[9] But even as Koo's ship steamed towards Europe, the Japanese and the government of Manchukuo finalised a deal under which Manchukuo's national security was handed over to the Japanese army to oversee. Manchukuo was, as Koo had predicted, now a staging post for Japanese troops on what had once been Chinese territory.

In the ensuing debates in Geneva, the Japanese cunningly dragged Koo personally into the issue by asking him whom he represented – Chiang Kai-shek or the warlord Zhang Xueliang. Koo's adversary in the League of Nations was Japan's Matsuoka Yōsuke (1880–1946), an American-educated diplomat who had once served as vice-consul in Shanghai. Matsuoka refused to accept any of the implied criticisms of the Lytton Report, leading Koo to remind him of the historical precedents for Japanese treachery and bullying. In particular, he reminded Matsuoka of the Twenty-One Demands and noted: *what Japan has done in the past in denying the authenticity of certain of her deeds, she may be doing again today.*[10]

Just as his predecessors had done in the case of Shandong at the Paris Peace Conference, Matsuoka asked the international community to seek 'peace based on realities' – in other words, to accept the establishment of Manchukuo as a *fait accompli.* Koo's response has strong echoes of his lifelong pursuit of justice, particularly in Paris: *Are we here to deal with realities alone and brush aside law and justice and the common interests of the peace of the world? Is this an organisation which recognises nothing but realities and which does not wish to uphold the principles of peace, law and justice upon which is it founded?*[11]

With Koo maintaining his customary eloquence in steering the Lytton Report through the committee stage, the Japanese lost many of the points they tried to raise. The international community sided with the Lytton Report, and with Wellington Koo's eloquent pursuit of justice. The representative for the Irish Free State resolved to stand with 'courage and determination' behind the rulings of the Report. Czechoslovakia agreed, and noted that Japan's attack on Shanghai could in no way be regarded as 'self-defence', despite Japanese claims to the contrary. Norway, Sweden and France offered their support, the latter with the additional note that no state within the League of Nations had the right to pursue redress by any method outside the peaceful methods set out in the League's own Covenant.

All the while, Matsuoka maintained that Japan had not violated any treaties. Eventually, he announced he was prepared to concede almost all of the Lytton Report's recommendations, except the League's refusal to recognise Manchukuo as an independent state under Japanese 'influence'. With some smaller powers calling for Japan to be expelled from the League, the recommendations of the Lytton Report were submitted for a vote. Japan voted against it and Siam abstained, whereas the other 42 nations present supported the Lytton recommendation that Manchukuo not be recognised as a state.

When the League, at Koo's urging, refused to budge, the Japanese made good on their long-held threat to walk out of the League. Unfortunately, the logistics of getting so many delegates out of the hall of the Assembly did not favour a swift and dramatic exit, forcing the Japanese to dawdle slowly out in ones and twos, while an enthusiastic Madame Koo, never afraid to show her feelings, applauded gleefully from the gallery.[12]

But it was a Pyrrhic victory for China. Although the League of Nations had voted in its favour, Japan was no longer in the room to hear the international community's censure. What use was the League of Nations if a country could walk out if it did not want to listen? Koo urged his fellow delegates to give serious thought to what the League might do to avert the crisis in Asia. *Shall they stand together*, he said, *to circumscribe, to control and speedily end it or shall they, drifting and disunited, be dragged one by one into what might so easily become a spreading whirlpool of disaster?*[13]

Koo himself had begun to question his faith in international intervention. China had waited for help in Manchuria and got nowhere, but when Chinese soldiers had engaged the Japanese in Shanghai, they had fought them to a standstill long enough to force a truce. Meanwhile, in the north, even as the League of Nations bickered over the next move, Japanese soldiers occupied the Shanhai Pass, the point where the Great Wall met the sea and the border of historical China. Instead of moving troops north to prevent further Japanese advances, Chiang Kai-shek continued a campaign against Communist insurgents far to the south.

In Geneva, Koo offered a warning to his fellow delegates. Japan's advance was unchecked, the League had done nothing to prevent it, just as the Paris Peace Conference had failed to fight for Shandong. *The situation*, he said, *brought the nations of the world to the point where the question to consider was how to save the League of Nations from destruction.*[14]

10

The Dark Clouds

Now Chinese ambassador to France, Koo tried to insinuate himself into Parisian high society, but continued to experience outbreaks of the subtle racism of indifference. For many in Europe, the conflict in China remained distant, and its participants were indistinguishable and interchangeable. At one lunch to which Koo had been invited, it soon became unpleasantly clear that the hostess believed he was the Japanese ambassador. 'Japan is a big power, becoming more powerful every day,' she enthused. 'You will surely be able to swallow up China.' Similarly, Madame Koo reported leaving a Parisian function and requesting the staff ring her driver to bring around her limousine. To red faces all round, the car that drew up was from the Japanese embassy, the hosts having called the Japanese in error, and the Japanese rushing to send a vehicle in the belief that they had lost their ambassador.[1]

Not all the problems came from the French side. A gendarme caught Koo's young sons throwing deck chairs into a lake in a Paris park. To what must have been their father's great embarrassment, the two boys tried to invoke diplomatic immunity.[2]

Japan continued to advance southwards, ostensibly in the interests of preserving the security of its puppet state of Manchukuo. *Although there has been no announcement of any change in policy,* Koo noted, *signs of the times seem to indicate that there has been a disinclination to pursue a policy of effective resistance – at any rate for the present. I believe that, if this is true, it will truly be a costly mistake in the end.*[3]

Koo's ally Zhang Xueliang, the Young Marshal, took matters into his own hands in a disastrous act on 12 December 1936, known as the Xi'an Incident. Frustrated with seeing his army wasting time and manpower in futile campaigns against Chinese Communists, Zhang resorted to drastic measures. In collaboration with another warlord, he kidnapped Chiang Kai-shek, hoping to persuade him by force that the Japanese were the true enemy, and that conflict with the Communists could wait. Although Zhang did force Chiang to agree to a united front against the Japanese, his act, which left Chiang shaken but unharmed, but cost the lives of several of Chiang's associates, would cost the Young Marshal his own career. Not long after Chiang Kai-shek was released, the Young Marshal was arrested; he would remain in custody for the next 57 years.

Although Zhang's methods were wildly misjudged, his behaviour showed how passionately many Chinese felt about the civil war between the Communists and the Nationalists, which distracted China from the true enemy in Japanese-occupied Manchuria. In 1937, a group of Japanese soldiers on exercises on the outskirts of Beijing demanded that a town under Chinese protection allow soldiers inside to look for a 'missing' member of the Japanese brigade. When the Chinese refused, the Japanese attacked, initiating a conflict over the boundary line between them, the Marco Polo Bridge, which soon escalated into a Japanese military advance, occupying Beijing and Tianjin. Although Japan and China had been skirmishing since 1931, the Chinese government had been reluctant to call the conflict a full-scale war, determined to deal with its own Communist insurgents before taking on the Japanese. However, the Marco Polo Bridge Incident represented the official outbreak of the Second Sino-Japanese War, which eventually merged into the Second World War.

Koo was disconsolate, writing: *I felt no face to see anybody. China became a joke.*[4] Despite his own mistrust of the Soviets, Koo urged Chiang Kai-shek to approach the USSR about a united front in Manchuria against the Japanese. The USSR, however, was unwilling to commit its troops to the Far East at that time. Instead, it offered military advisers and equipment to China, in the hope that China would hold Japan back on its behalf.

> The aggression of Japan on China was flagrant and if the League should refuse to take cognizance of it, the League would be a complete farce.
>
> **WELLINGTON KOO**

Wearily, Koo went back to the League of Nations, with stories of an actual Japanese invasion, not of Manchuria, but of China itself. *The aggression of Japan on China was flagrant*, he observed, *and if the League should refuse to take cognizance of it, the League would be a complete farce.*[5]

On 15 September, Koo made a damning speech to the League Council, in which he deliberately enumerated Japanese atrocities in a context of foreign observers: *In [Tianjin], the most crowded parts of the Chinese city were bombed by Japanese aeroplanes killing hundreds of people at a time for no reason other than to terrorize the civilians. The sight of the mangled bodies and the cries of the maimed and wounded were so sickening to the hearts of the foreign Red Cross doctors that they voiced their fervent wish that the Governments of the civilised Powers would make an effort to stop the carnage.*[6]

Koo's long list of atrocities was carefully chosen, not for the horrors it contained, but for its direct links to foreigners – these events happened under the eyes of overseas observers, and had been catalogued not by the Chinese, but by Europeans. He read from a report in the London *Daily Mail* that spoke of an attack on a train full of refugees, and noted that the location was close to the French Concession in Shanghai. He spoke of an artillery bombardment on a university, and accused the Japanese of using Shanghai's International Settlement, the home of most of the city's European ex-pats, as a base for their military operations. He even alluded, without naming the individual or country, to a Japanese aerial attack against an ambassador from a *great and friendly Power.*

Koo noted, for the benefit of any Japanese sympathisers, that not even Japan's excuses could be trusted. Even for those who thought Japan deserved 'Lebensraum' in Manchuria, he noted that Japan's supposed over-population was clearly not as bad as the Japanese had alleged. If it were, he noted, surely Japanese immigrants would have been arriving in Formosa (Taiwan) in larger numbers over the preceding 40 years, or indeed in Korea since it had become a Japanese colony. Nor did Koo see any justification in the argument that Japan 'needed' raw materials – Japan already had ample imports from the United States, India, Malaya, Australia, Canada and others. His list of trading partners was a return to his earlier rhetoric, a means of forcing the international community to confront the actions of Japan as something that was inextricably linked to them. Koo also warned that the international community stood to lose out, as well.

This statement is not made here with a view to alarming you, lied Koo, *but ... European and American interests are already feeling the menace ... . If Japan should succeed ... the end of the vast commercial interests there of Europe and America could be easily foreseen.*[7]

As Koo saw it, China was fighting not only for self-preservation, but *to safeguard the rights and interests of the foreign Powers within her borders.* Koo predicted that a Japanese victory against China would soon lead to Japanese moves against any remaining foreign interests. Quoting once again from a foreign source, the British Foreign Secretary Anthony Eden, he called a Japanese blockade *as illegal as it is inhuman.* Quoting the US Secretary of State, he noted that it was a situation *in which the rights and interests of all nations ... may be affected.* He finished by quoting the League's own Covenant, that *Any war or threat of war ... is ... a matter of concern to the whole League.*[8]

Koo's speech to the League was his last effort to drag the international community into honouring the undertakings it had given at Paris and Washington, but owed less to treaties than direct appeal to the Powers' own sense of safety. China, warned Koo, was only the current victim; if the international community failed to act, then they might be next. He reiterated this warning in a broadcast to the American people on 26 September 1937: *The one dominant purpose of the Japanese military party is to make Japan the warlord of Eastern Asia and the mistress of the Pacific. The achievement of this purpose is considered as an essential step to the eventual realisation of Japan's so-called mission to dominate the world. Force is their chosen instrument to carry out their policy.*

International law, treaty obligations, and humanitarian con-
siderations which all peace-loving and civilised people desire
to uphold, mean nothing to them.[9]

Koo's own government had ordered him to push for sanctions against Japan, which he did not believe was a likely
outcome from the League. Meanwhile, US representatives
had warned him off any claim that the US might help broker
a deal between China and Japan. The best that the League
could do, following the lead of the British representative, was
to call for yet another conference, this time to discuss the
implications of the Nine Power Treaty. For Koo, this passing
of the buck and further wasting of time was crushing news.
The proposal fell like a bomb, deafening all senses.[10]

Koo set off for Brussels for the conference, on a journey
which took him through fields and towns who sheer newness
spoke of the immense damage wrought on the region by the
First World War. *The world had learned little from it*, he
wrote. *A new war was in the atmosphere everywhere.*[11]

Japan refused to send representatives to Brussels, instead
sending a note that it 'could not do otherwise than maintain
its previously expressed point of view that the present action
of Japan in her relations with China was a measure of self-
defence and did not come within the scope of the Nine Power
Treaty'.[12]

The assembled nations at Brussels, a veritable re-run of the
Powers at the Paris Peace Conference, with the addition of the
USSR, begged to differ. With the Japanese absent, the Brussels Conference ruled that the Japanese action was indeed in
contravention of the Nine Power Treaty, in a long statement
that said the same thing over and over again, wringing meta-
phorical hands about Japan having broken the terms, that the
Conference did not like it, but that without Japan's willing

cooperation in the Conference, it was unclear what should be done.

Many delegates admitted it was a shambles. Sweden, Norway and Denmark abstained from signing the Conference report. Italy actively voted against the report, citing it as 'a door open not towards the settlement of the conflict, but rather towards more serious complications'.[13]

On 12 December 1937, as Japanese forces took control of Nanjing, many defenders, including the remnants of Chiang Kai-shek's government, fled upriver. The 'Republic of China' now fought with its back to the mountains, from its new provisional capital in Chongqing. Meanwhile, the American gunboat *Panay*, aiding the evacuation of American personnel, sought refuge from the fighting by steaming upriver. The Japanese navy was aware of its presence, causing its officers to question an order to sink any vessels upriver of Nanjing. The order, however, was confirmed, and Japanese planes sank the *Panay*, with the loss of three lives and with 48 crew and civilian casualties.

Many, including Koo, thought that the *Panay* incident would bring other countries into the Sino-Japanese War. The *Panay* had been flying large American flags, and had another painted on the top of her superstructure. The British government actually began the process of moving warships to the region, only for Japan to offer apologies, unlikely excuses and a $2 million indemnity. Koo commented that *the dark clouds blew over without breaking into a storm.*[14]

Instead, China got some unofficial support from some of the Powers. The USSR was already supplying military aid to Chiang Kai-shek. The British built the Burma Road in Indo-China to get supplies to Chiang's forces in the hinterland. All the while, Koo pressed for some form of better action from the League of Nations, although in the end, it passed little more than a resolution calling for 'specially interested' powers to consult with other 'similarly interested' powers. *It would have been better*, commented Koo, *to have no resolution at all if this was the best that could be obtained.*[15]

In March 1938, Hitler's move on Austria led to closer ties between Germany and Japan. German assistance to China was cut off, and the drift of Europe towards its own war threatened to deprive the Chinese of further support against Japan. The Munich peace conference, of September 1938, seemed to offer Hitler the same kind of appeasement that had been offered to Japan in China. While Neville Chamberlain promised 'peace in our time' to the British, Koo commented to his superiors in China that the resolutions of the League were *nothing but empty words.*[16]

∞∞∞

For much of the Second World War, Wellington Koo was a Chinese ambassador, at first in France, and then, following the Nazi invasion, in Great Britain. According to Madame Koo's autobiography, it was in Paris that Wellington Koo began to conduct an open affair with Juliana Young, the wife of an embassy staffer. An exasperated Madame Koo eventually pulled strings to have the woman's husband assigned to a new post. He was packed off to a posting in the Philippines, in which capacity he was later executed by the Japanese. Madame Koo's rival, however, was reunited with Koo after the war.[17]

The Koo family fled for Bordeaux ahead of the Nazi invasion, and lost a significant portion of their belongings when a stray bomb hit a cargo truck. 'Wellington's beloved fishing tackle, which he had treasured for twenty years, was destroyed,' wrote Madame Koo. In Bordeaux itself, the Koo family arrived shortly in advance of a large-scale bombing raid, which shook the hotel. Koo himself sat with agitated composure in a chair in the lobby, while a French general dove for cover. The general, who had recently come from the front lines, apologised for his panicked behaviour.[18]

Despite a status bordering on that of a refugee, Koo continued to represent China. Neutral Portugal was celebrating its 300th anniversary. He and his staff undertook a gruelling train journey through Spain to Lisbon, arriving after over twelve hours of delays to find nobody waiting on the platform. He was, however, recognised as Chinese by two aviators, who saluted and asked: 'We have heard so much about the Wellington Koos [*sic*] who are supposed to represent China at the celebration. Do you know them, or by any chance could you be Ambassador Koo yourself?'[19]

Soon after his return to France, Koo took up a new residence in Vichy, under impoverished conditions that required him, for what Madame Koo archly observed may have been the first time in his life, to cook for himself using tinned food in his cramped quarters. Koo's austerity was, however, at least partly self-imposed. As an ambassador, he could have exploited his rank to get luxury food items, but would have been ill at ease keeping them for himself. Nor was it likely that the food would arrive in large enough quantities to be satisfactorily divided among Koo's dozen staff – consequently, Koo preferred to go without.[20]

Koo lasted in Vichy for as long as there was a semblance of French autonomy in matters of foreign policy. After the Vichy government agreed to Nazi demands over the disposition of Indo-China in September 1940, there was little for Koo to do.

When the Chinese Ambassador to Great Britain was recalled to become a Foreign Minister to Chiang Kai-shek in Chongqing, Koo was moved to the London post. He sent Madame Koo to New York, despite her protestations, for her safety. She would only return to London with him two years later, shortly after he was forced to quash her attempt to publish her autobiography.

In the aftermath of Pearl Harbor, Koo was able to push for better cooperation between the British, Americans and Chinese. He secured from the British Foreign Minister Anthony Eden a promise to relinquish many of the remaining rights acquired through the Unequal Treaties after the Opium Wars

China's position as one of the Allied Powers gave Koo greater sway at the Dumbarton Oaks Conference of 1944 – Chiang Kai-shek had argued with Roosevelt that 'without the participation of the Asiatic peoples, the conference will have no meaning for half of humanity'.[21] As a delegate at Dumbarton Oaks, Koo suggested the formation of a 'world federation of states', with each state's political power determined by the size of its population.

In the wake of the German surrender in 1945, Koo formed one of China's ten delegates at the United Nations Conference on International Organization at San Francisco. The Conference established many of the guidelines and institutions of what would become the United Nations Organization after the defeat of Japan, and Koo's presence ensured that he contributed several proposals to the draft constitution of the UN. It was, for example, Wellington Koo who proposed that *if any party to a dispute fails to comply with the judgement of the International Court of Justice, the Security Council may, upon application by the other party or parties concerned, take such action as it may deem necessary to give effect to the judgement.* Such a clause, if adopted, would give the Security Council of the UN the power to enforce decisions made by its international court, and slice through the kind of delaying tactics and smokescreens that had been employed by the Japanese over the previous decades.

Koo's proposal met with strong objections from the US, USSR and Britain, the Security Council member nations who would then be obliged by such a clause to suborn their foreign policies to the will of an international court. Koo enjoyed greater success with an amendment that proposed: *in the case of a non-member, it should be required to accept for the purpose of such dispute, the obligations of pacific settlement provided in the Charter.*[22] Such a clause, it was hoped, would ensure that even those countries that might not be members of the United Nations (as the US had not been of the League of Nations), would be obliged to abide by its decisions if they sought its adjudication.

With the arrival of France, late, to the Conference, there were now five main powers – China, the USSR, the US, the UK and France, comprising what would eventually become the permanent members of the UN Security Council. As the various foreign ministers returned home and left the minutiae to their deputies, Koo appointed himself to the Chinese committee and stayed on in San Francisco.

In the committee stage, Koo pushed for a clause in the UN Charter that promoted *the development toward independence or self-government as may be appropriate to the particular circumstance of each territory and its people.* This met with opposition from those powers such as Britain that still had colonies, as it implied that the UN was dedicated to dismantling all colonies. Determined to ensure broad support for the draft Charter of the UN, Koo also asked that the smaller nations be given more time to peruse it, to ensure that they knew what they were signing to, and did so happily.

On 26 June 1945, with war still raging in the Pacific, the Conference concluded with the signing of the Charter by the members present. In recognition of the fact that China had been the first of the United Nations to be attacked by an Axis power (in either 1928, or 1931, or 1937, depending on where one drew the line on Japanese intrigues), Koo was given the honour of being the first to sign. He was back in the US barely two months later, having been moved from his embassy in Britain to the US, where he was expected to be the Chinese Ambassador to Washington, and also to oversee the early days of the United Nations

11
The Divided Nations

On 15 August 1945, the day of Japan's surrender, Koo wrote in his diary: *At last the moment to which I had been looking forward and about which I had dreamed and worked has arrived.*[1] His elation, however, at the defeat of Japan was short-lived. China's efforts to throw off Japanese aggression, which had occupied the country and Koo for 50 years, had left both weak. Soon after the Second World War, Koo was sent to America to negotiate American aid for China, and he would eventually serve a decade in Washington as China's ambassador. 'China', however, was a dwindling concept – Chiang Kai-shek's government had moved from Nanjing to Chongqing, and then to Taiwan as Communist revolutionaries took control of the country. Koo counselled swift diplomatic discussion with the Soviet Union, sufficient to cut off the supplies of Soviet aid to the Communists. This, in turn, Koo argued, would put the Communists and his own Nationalists on a more equal footing, and allow for talks to begin over settling their differences and bringing peace back to China. *No nation can be strong unless it is united*, he said. *In the test of power politics of the modern post-war world,*

China could not play her part without a unified government and army.[2]

However, Koo was thwarted in his aims. In the case of post-Second World War China, the interference of the Great Powers had taken on a new form, that of contention by proxy. The Soviet-backed Communists and the American-backed Nationalists were soon at each other's throats, but with the Communists enjoying a much stronger position. Chiang Kai-shek refused to trust his Communist 'allies', who were only on his side briefly for the duration of their joint opposition to Japan.

Koo arrived in America determined to help the Nationalists win back China by gaining greater American support. He hoped to capitalise on Chiang Kai-shek's position at the end of the war as one of America's allies, and to educate the Americans about China. Koo planned a massive cultural offensive, aimed largely at thwarting the kind of ignorance he had faced in Europe, encouraging the Americans to think of the Chinese as their friends. Although he would deny it, his activities amounted to the formation of a China Lobby, designed to put thoughts of China in American minds during the period of reconstruction, and to ensure that American public opinion favoured Chiang Kai-shek and the Nationalists.

Koo's allies in this endeavour included the likes of Madame Chiang Kai-shek, who had been educated in Georgia and had already charmed America during the war with her Southern Belle accent. His soft approach, he hoped, would ensure that enough goodwill towards America would be forthcoming. This was particularly important considering the Nationalists' lack of success in China itself. By the end of the 1940s, the administration Koo served only ruled a small island in the south-west, and China's effective ruler was Chairman Mao.

The proclamation of the People's Republic (PRC) put Koo in a difficult position. The beleaguered Republic of China (ROC), occupied with its mass retreat to Taiwan, had other things on its collective mind, forcing Koo and his staff to work without pay. The early 1950s were dominated by posturing from both the Nationalist government on Taiwan, and the Communist government on the mainland, that China would be reunited by military force. In a cost-cutting measure, an ROC politician tried to reduce the number of embassies abroad, leading Koo to deliver an impassioned plea to keep diplomatic channels open.

Mao Zedong (1893–1976) was raised in Hunan, far upriver from Koo's birthplace in cosmopolitan Shanghai. A farmer's son, Mao had a traditional Chinese education, which was rendered irrelevant by the abolition of the imperial examination system. Mao discovered Communism while studying and working in Beijing, and is remembered, a trifle misleadingly, as one of the founders of the Chinese Communist Party. As Party leader, he enjoyed a special authority, even on occasions when he held no post in government. He proclaimed the People's Republic of China – i.e. Communist rule – from the Gate of Heavenly Peace (*Tiananmen*) in Beijing in 1949.

The Nationalist government, having lost the mainland and having established itself on a small island, had, as its only hope of maintaining itself as an international entity in the family of nations, to keep up its international relations and cultivate the friendship of the non-Communist world, so that when the time came for Taiwan to launch a campaign for the recovery of the mainland, we could count upon its sympathy and support ... [3]

Even so, Koo remained cautious. With the outbreak of the Korean War in 1950, Chiang Kai-shek immediately saw the potential to push the United Nations actions over the Yalu River and into China proper, perhaps even smuggling the opening salvoes of the retaking of the mainland in under the auspices of a UN police action. Koo, however, agreed with the US Department of State that committing Chinese troops to Korea risked turning a local issue into an international one, and effectively re-igniting the Second World War. Koo made the offer anyway, to General Douglas MacArthur, presumably in the knowledge that MacArthur would follow his superiors' policy and decline with thanks.

One of Koo's new diplomatic problems was the legal status of Taiwan itself. Although claimed as Chinese territory, the island had been handed over to Japan as part of the settlement of the first Sino-Japanese war of 1895. Japan was now under US occupation, but the terms of a final peace treaty were still under negotiation. The earlier Cairo Agreement had established that Formosa (Taiwan) and the Pescadores islands between the island and the mainland would be restored to the government of China, but the 'government of China' was, once more, in dispute between two factions.

The 'liberation' of Taiwan by the Allies was a mixed blessing. Chiang Kai-shek insisted it was and always had been part of China, but faced opposition from locals who had been sympathetic to the ousted Japanese, and native Formosans who wanted independence. Clashes between the new arrivals and the locals led to the imposition of martial law that lasted until 1987. Some two million of Chiang Kai-shek's followers fled to the island in 1949, for what was originally intended as a temporary retreat. The new arrivals swamped the indigenous population, and their descendants remain there to this day. Taiwan is still the last bastion of the 'Republican' Chinese.

Koo's campaign to keep Chiang Kai-shek's government in America's good books became more difficult in the face of the Communist gains on the mainland. With the Taiwanese regime accused of corruption, atrocities and mismanagement, Koo found it difficult to present the Nationalists in a

good light. *We cannot hope to pull the wool over peoples'
eyes by ignoring such questions*, he wrote. *Why did our four
million troops not fight the Com[munists] with favourable
odds of 10–1 in number and with added advantages of an air
force and navy? Why did we not manage our finances better
to forestall the collapse of our own currency? Why did the
people refuse to support the Gov't?*[4]

As the post-war environment transformed into the early
days of the Cold War, Koo enjoyed better success by avoiding
discussion of the Nationalists' failings, and instead pointing
out that they were the best chance that the capitalist world
had of avoiding a Communist China. To do so, he would
need to avoid giving the impression that Taiwan was a one-
party dictatorship under martial law. Despite a life lived in
an eternal avoidance of party politics, Koo suggested the
formation of the Chinese Liberal Party, in order to present
politics on Taiwan with the argument and debate that the
Americans wanted to see in a healthy democracy. However,
he had trouble finding support for the scheme – Chinese students returning from America regarded the Guomindang as
the only party that would advance their careers, and were
unwilling to form an opposition merely to placate hypotheti-
cal American supporters.

Instead, Koo's position as American ambassador came
under fire. Some regarded his efforts for cleaner government
on Taiwan as a veiled attack on Chiang Kai-shek himself.
Koo protested that he was merely trying to get the Republic
off a war footing and into peaceful, civilian life. That would
involve using schools to teach children instead of quartering
troops; not using the military to put down public demonstrations, lifting martial law, and, of course, permitting an opposition. Stories of corruption in the Nationalist government

also came to taint Koo by association, as if by serving the Nationalists, he had to be on the take himself. None of this helped in the argument over which Chinese government Taiwan should be 'returned' to. In fact, in the 1950s just as in the 21st century, the sole thing that the Nationalists and the Communists could agree on was that Taiwan *was* part of China. The argument, as it was and still is, focused on who had the right to claim to rule Taiwan, when the ROC ruled nothing but, and the PRC ruled everything else.

The first attempt to have the ROC ousted from its seat on the Security Council came as early as 1950, when the Soviets staged a protest for several months, claiming that Koo did not have the right to speak for mainland China. In fact, Koo claimed to speak for all China, just as the Communists did.

This impasse allowed for some cunning diplomacy from the Chinese over the presence of American warships in the strait between Taiwan and the mainland. Although it was widely understood that the US presence was there to prevent a Communist invasion of Taiwan, nowhere was it established that Taiwan was a foreign country that could be 'invaded'. John Foster Dulles feared that too close an examination of this issue might lead the Communists to use the terms of non-intervention treaties, ironically established in many cases by Koo himself, to argue that the American presence in the strait was an illegal interference in an internal Chinese matter, and hence a violation of China's territorial integrity. Technically, preventing an invasion of Taiwan could be interpreted as an infringement of the UN Charter which Koo himself had signed – an argument which was in fact offered in August 1950 by Zhou Enlai.[5]

Meanwhile, Japan's pre-war occupation of Taiwan needed to come to an official end. The Japanese had already agreed to leave, but the question remained as to whom they should officially hand over. In consultation with John Foster Dulles, Koo agreed that it would be in everyone's interests to simply pursue an official renunciation of Japan's claim on Taiwan, and to worry about who actually inherited the island later. However, for as long as the Communists were the *de facto* rulers of the bulk of Chinese territory, it might prove difficult to allow the ROC to sign any treaties on behalf of China. Koo argued that it was the Nationalists who had waged the war against the Japanese, and who had participated in the various conferences and councils to arrange the terms of the peace. This was true, although it did ignore the presence of innumerable Communist insurgents fighting the Japanese – part of the reason for the Communists' swift advances after 1945 was that to many isolated communities, Communist guerrillas were the only anti-Japanese forces they had seen for years.

Regardless, the peace treaty was signed in 1952, more than 20 years after Japanese soldiers had blown up 31 inches of railway in Mukden. The deadlock remained over which China Japan was negotiating with. In answer to the American concerns about who spoke for mainland China, and also in recognition of the widespread belief at the time that the ROC's Taiwan exile was only a temporary setback, the wording allowed: 'the terms of the present treaty shall, in respect of the Republic of China, be applicable to all the territories which are now, or which may hereafter be, under the control of the Government'.[6]

The Korean War, and the part played in it by Communist China, was to serve Taiwan's interests very well. It led to an American decision to offer a 14-year military aid package, sufficient to keep the Communists from crossing the strait to retake Taiwan by force. It also led to a United Nations motion, proposed by Great Britain, that the issue of whether the ROC had the right to speak for all China should be postponed for a decade.

Although this left the ROC safe for the time being in the United Nations, its presence on other international bodies was slowly eroded. Koo blamed Chiang Kai-shek for this, and his insistence on withdrawing from any organisation that offered membership to Communist China. *Better to face expulsion and protest against it*, warned Koo, *than voluntarily withdraw for fear of sure expulsion in [the] end.*[7] Moreover, Koo felt that his propaganda campaign was limited by lack of funding, and complained that Pakistan and South Korea spent more money currying favour with the American media than the Republic of China.

The ROC's position continued to diminish. In 1954, Communist attacks on a handful of islands close to the mainland coast went largely unanswered by the American defenders who were supposedly in the Taiwan Straits to protect the ROC's interests. Already in Washington, there was a lobby that pushed for recognition of the state things as they were, *res sic stantibus*, which was that there were now two Chinas, the People's Republic on the mainland and the Republic on Taiwan, and that they were effectively separate states. Chiang refused to listen to such suggestions, but faced more challenges in the years that followed.

In 1955, one of Koo's earlier diplomatic arguments returned to haunt him after 20 years. Outer Mongolia, still coloured-in as part of China on ROC maps, was admitted to the United Nations as a member state. The deal was brokered between the US and the Soviet Union, each agreeing to recognise satellites and allies of the other in the United Nations.

Chiang Kai-shek refused to let the incident pass, and Koo was obliged to use China's veto on the Security Council. He did so bitterly, noting that: *the real difficulty of the free world … was the lack of a firm stand on the part of the free world in dealing with Communism.*[8]

It was, however, a ludicrous state of affairs. Koo's government laid claim to Outer Mongolia, even though it had been a separate entity for decades, and had in fact been given up already, at least twice. The powers at the United Nations hoped that Koo would not veto, because doing so would make it clear how little right the ROC had to claim to speak for China, and yet Koo was obliged to do. It was difficult, then as now, to see much difference between the 'independence' of Mongolia under Soviet influence and the 'independence' of Manchuria 20 years earlier under the Japanese.

> **The real difficulty of the free world … was the lack of a firm stand on the part of the free world in dealing with Communism.**
> **WELLINGTON KOO**

By 1956, it was all over. The United States began talks with Communist China in the hope of securing an agreement to resolve the conflict over Taiwan by peaceful means. Even if this led to a solution, it implied that the United States was prepared to deal with Communist China as a legitimate government. The idea of 'two Chinas', which would become part of the rhetoric of *détente* in the Nixon era, was already taking shape.

The circumstances of Koo's resignation as ambassador are confusing. He had already tried to leave the diplomatic service at the end of the Korean War, but had been refused. Four years later, he was tired from decades of political arguments, and was estranged from his third wife, whose wealth had probably been invaluable in supporting him through the times when his own country could not afford to pay his salary. Much of Koo's personal wealth, in buildings and real estate, was now lost in Communist China. He felt that he, like the administration he served, was no longer being treated as the representative of a quarter of the world's population, but merely as a functionary from an obscure Pacific island. Worst of all, he felt *one could not see the results of one's effort, whereas in other fields one could feel one was building something and in [the] course of time could see it function.*[9]

In 1956, Koo was called to Taiwan for a meeting at short notice, and returned to curtly announce to his wife that he was resigning. Despite this ominous procession of events, it was understood that he was resigning on account of his old age – he was, after all, nearing 70. Even so, there were strong efforts to retain his services. John Foster Dulles, who had first met Koo at the Paris Peace Conference, was now the US Secretary of State, and so unwilling to see him retire that he even offered to persuade the government in Taiwan to refuse Koo's resignation. Koo was offered a sinecure post of Ambassador at Large, which he also refused. He accepted a position as Senior Adviser on Foreign Affairs to Chiang Kai-shek, but resigned from that post after only a few months to accept a new responsibility.

The death of a Chinese judge at the International Court of Justice at The Hague left an opening for a Chinese national with legal experience who could command international respect. Reasoning that a judge's job was less taxing than an ambassador's, Koo agreed to stand for the post. His main competitor for the office was a Japanese official, but Koo gained a unanimous vote in the second round. He served out the remaining months of his predecessor's term, and was then re-elected for another ten-year tenure. For his last three years in that post, he was the Vice President of the International Court of Justice.[10]

As the 1960s came to a close, Koo was approached by Taipei with a request to run again – it was believed that he was the only figure from Republican China who stood a chance of maintaining Taipei's presence on the International Court of Justice. However, President Lyndon B Johnson had already promised the seat to the Philippines, and Taipei withdrew its request. Koo's last diplomatic act, then, was arguably to step aside in favour of a Filipino successor in 1967, thereby guaranteeing the Philippines' support for Taiwan at the United Nations. This, however, did not work for long – regardless of what good graces Koo may have earned for his country, the Republic of China lost its permanent seat on the UN Security Council, forced to hand it over to the *People's* Republic of China, which the UN finally acknowledged as the *de facto* ruler of most Chinese territory. The concept of a republican mainland China on the world stage, to which Koo had dedicated his entire career, now effectively ceased to exist.

Wellington Koo lived out the remaining years of his life in retirement in New York – his hometown of Shanghai was now under Communist control, as was the site of his palatial Beijing residence. He had no desire to retire to Taiwan, an island that he had not even visited until after the Nationalist retreat there. He remained a pillar of the overseas Chinese community, gaining the questionable distinction late in life of inspiring the creation of a Chinese recipe, Cabbage Wellington, named in his honour by the chef Virginia Lee. He presented his academic papers to Columbia University in 1963, and participated in an Oral History project at his old university that resulted in the preservation of several hundred hours of his reminiscences. In 1972, amid the intrigues of Nixon and Kissinger to win a rapprochement with Communist China, Koo was one of the dignitaries invited to Beijing by Chairman Mao in an attempt to demonstrate his change in attitudes. Koo declined the invitation.

On Koo's death, many of his obituaries repeated a phrase that has come to characterise his diplomatic career, cited in an issue of *Time* magazine on the eve of the outbreak of the Second World War. It contains much of Koo's attitude for his whole career from Paris onwards – true words spoken with biting wit but a sense of melancholy resignation. *The recent history of Europe and Asia shows beyond a doubt the futility of trying to turn a tiger into a kitten by giving it a dish of cream.*[11]

Notes

Introduction

1. S Bonsal, *Suitors and Suppliants: The Little Nations at Versailles* (Prentice Hall, New York: 1946) p 236.
2. Bonsal, *Suitors and Suppliants*, p 239.

1: The Unequal Treaties

1. Madame Wellington [Hui-lan] Koo, with Mary van Rensselaer Thayer, *Hui-lan Koo: An Autobiography* (Dial Press, New York: 1943) p 125, hereafter *Hui-lan Koo*. We may presume that Madame Koo's recollections are derived from Wellington himself, although her dates, presumably filtered through her American amanuenses, are occasionally slightly off. She claims, for example, that Wellington was 16 when he finished at St John's – this is true by Chinese reckoning, which counts one's date of birth as one's 'first' birthday, but not in Anglo-American orthography.
2. Madame Wellington [Hui-lan] Koo, with Isabella Taves, *No Feast Lasts Forever* (Quadrangle Books, New York: 1975) pp 113–14, hereafter *No Feast Lasts Forever*; *Hui-lan Koo*, p 114 – both discreetly refuse to name the

luckless girl. P Chu, *V.K. Wellington Koo: A Study of the Diplomat and Diplomacy of Warlord China, During His Early Career, 1919–1924*. Doctoral dissertation, University of Pennsylvania, 1971, hereafter Chu, *V. K. Wellington Koo* (a), gives the surname Zhang (Chang), p 20n, and subsequently in *V.K. Wellington Koo: A Case Study of China's Diplomat and Diplomacy of Nationalism 1912–1966* (Chinese University Press, Hong Kong: 1981) p 5n, hereafter Chu, *V. K. Wellington Koo* (b). The Chinese-language version of Wikipedia is more forthcoming, naming the father as Zhang Yunxiang and the daughter as Zhang Run'e.

3. V K Tung, *V K. Wellington Koo and China's Wartime Diplomacy* (Center of Asian Studies, St John's University, New York: 1977) p 86, hereafter Tung, *Wartime Diplomacy*. Koo wrote those words 50 years later, on 15 August 1945, the day of Japan's final surrender.

4. M Macmillan, *Paris 1919* (Random House, New York: 2001) p 326.

5. Chu, *V.K. Wellington Koo* (a), p 28; Chu, *V.K. Wellington Koo* (b), p 9.

2: The Open Door

1. Koo, *Reminiscences*, quoted in Chu, *V.K. Wellington Koo* (b), pp 5–6.

2. S Craft, *V.K. Wellington Koo and the Emergence of Modern China* (University Press of Kentucky, Lexington: 2004) p 9, hereafter Craft, *V. K. Wellington Koo*. It is fascinating to compare Koo's educational experience, and his reaction to it, with that of another

Confucian scholar upriver: see J Clements, *Mao Zedong* (Haus Publishing, London: 2006) pp 3–4.

3. Chu, *V.K. Wellington Koo* (b), p 6 claims Koo edited the student newspaper, which he calls *Dragon*, although his source for this is a page in *Hui-lan Koo*. Craft, *V.K. Wellington Koo*, claims that the newspaper was called the *St John's Echo*, and the school year book was called *Dragon Flag*.

4. *Hui-lan Koo*, p 126.

5. I have limited my claims for Koo's Columbia achievements to those described in Columbia University's own online biography, and those that Koo claimed for himself in direct interviews. There is a wealth of other alleged achievements, although some seem based on Hui-lan Koo's unreliable memory of things her husband may have mentioned in passing. Chu, *V.K. Wellington Koo* (b), p 7, claims that Koo organised the 'Chinese Students Alliance in America', although this was established in 1901 at the University of California at Berkeley, when Koo was still a 13-year-old schoolboy! It seems more likely that Koo was instrumental in a grand union of Chinese student associations in 1911, and was probably among the founders of the Chinese Students' Association of the Eastern States. See H Lai, 'The Chinese-Marxist Left, Chinese students and scholars in America, and the New China: mid-1940s to mid-1950s,' in *Chinese America: History and Perspectives*, 1 January 2004 (online). Note that although he completed his bachelor's degree in 1908, Koo withheld his diploma fee until 1909 in order to graduate alongside his classmates, by which time his Master's studies were well underway.

6. Koo, *Diary*, quoted in Craft, *V.K. Wellington Koo*, p 23.
7. V Koo, *The Status of Aliens in China* (Columbia University, New York: 1912) pp 7–8.
8. Craft, *V.K. Wellington Koo*, p 33.

3: The Twenty-One Demands

1. R Fifield, *Woodrow Wilson and the Far East: The Diplomacy of the Shantung Question* (Thomas Y Crowell Company, New York: 1952) p 25.
2. E Selle, *Donald of China* (Harper and Brothers, New York: 1948) p 159. It is, of course, difficult to see how China could use the Japanese threats to 'save face' when the Japanese were so keen to keep the threats secret.
3. Selle, *Donald of China*, p 168. Selle claims that it was Donald, later the shadowy figure behind Zhang Xueliang, who drafted China's reply to the Japanese.
4. Fifield, *Woodrow Wilson and the Far East*, p 48.
5. W M Hughes, letter to Russell Fifield, quoted in Fifield, *Woodrow Wilson and the Far East*, pp 60–1. As far as Hughes was concerned, the chilling implication was that, having seized the Carolines, Japan would have happily allied with Germany and attacked Australia if Britain had not made promises to let Japan hang onto the islands in the post-war peace.
6. Craft, *V.K. Wellington Koo*, p 38.
7. T Lu [Lu Zhengxiang], *Ways of Confucius and of Christ* (Burns Oates, London: 1948) p 38.
8. Craft, *V.K. Wellington Koo*, p 43.
9. Fifield, *Woodrow Wilson and the Far East*, p 712.
10. 'China: The Early Republican Period,' on *Encyclopaedia Britannica DVD-ROM*.
11. Chu, *V.K. Wellington Koo* (b), p 15.

4: Musical Chairs

1. Letter from Koo to John Bassett Moore, quoted in Craft, *V.K. Wellington Koo*, p 45.

2. Koo, *Wunsz King Collection*, quoted in Chu, *V.K. Wellington Koo* (b), p 16.

3. Craft, *V.K. Wellington Koo*, p 49; Chu, *V.K. Wellington Koo* (b), p 16 makes it clear that even at their 1918 meeting, Wilson tried to tell Koo that the Fourteen Points 'would probably be more difficult to apply to the Far East'.

4. W King, *Woodrow Wilson, Wellington Koo and the China Question at the Paris Peace Conference* (A W Sythoff, Leyden: 1959) p 7, hereafter King, *Woodrow Wilson, Wellington Koo*.

5. Chu, *V.K. Wellington Koo* (b), p 14. At least two of the south's preferred representatives travelled to Paris anyway as private citizens, and undoubtedly stirred things up during the Conference. Wu Chaoshu was sent as an official emissary from Canton, but failed to insinuate himself into the delegation. Wang Jingwei (a.k.a. Wang Zhaoming), who would later find infamy as a Japanese quisling, was one of the anti-American agitators who so troubled Stephen Bonsal in May, and delivered a 'moving' speech about 'the despair to which the people would be reduced when they heard of the [Shandong] betrayal ... ' See Bonsal, *Suitors and Suppliants*, p 243.

6. N Keegan, 'From Chancery to Cloister: The Chinese Diplomat Who Became a Benedictine Monk,' in *Diplomacy and Statecraft*, Vol 10, No 1 (March 1999) p 177.

7. E T Williams, head of the Far East Division in the State Department, quoted in Fifield, *Woodrow Wilson and the Far East*, p 183; Bonsal, *Suitors and Suppliants*, p 237.

8. Fifield, *Woodrow Wilson and the Far East*, p 144.

9. Fifield, *Woodrow Wilson and the Far East*, p 183.

10. C Pearl, *Morrison of Peking* (Penguin Australia, Victoria: 1970) pp 373–4.

11. Chu, *V.K. Wellington Koo* (b), p 17.

12. Fifield, *Woodrow Wilson and the Far East*, p 187.

13. Pearl, *Morrison of Peking*, p 380.

5: Cat and Mouse

1. Fifield, *Woodrow Wilson and the Far East*, p 126.

2. Fifield, *Woodrow Wilson and the Far East*, p 125.

3. Fifield, *Woodrow Wilson and the Far East*, p 127, claims that C T Wang made the request. King, *Woodrow Wilson, Wellington Koo*, p 8, claims it was Koo.

4. King, *Woodrow Wilson, Wellington Koo*, p 8.

5. Fifield, *Woodrow Wilson and the Far East*, pp 140–2. The information was unknown to the Chinese at the time, and was presented by Makino in a secret report after the Conference, which has since been declassified.

6. Fifield, *Woodrow Wilson and the Far East*, p 192.

7. G Clemenceau, *Grandeur and Misery of Victory* (George Harrap, London: 1930) p 140.

8. Macmillan, *Paris 1919*, p 334.

9. King, *Woodrow Wilson, Wellington Koo*, p 9.

10. Lu, *Ways of Confucius and of Christ*, p 40. Notably, Lu claims that he deliberately selected Koo to speak for him at the session. Although Lu is normally written off as an ineffectual diplomat, he may simply have been wise in knowing when to delegate.

11. Bonsal, *Suitors and Suppliants*, p 235.

12. King, *Woodrow Wilson, Wellington Koo*, p 12.

13. Fifield, *Woodrow Wilson and the Far East*, p 177.

14. Fifield, *Woodrow Wilson and the Far East*, p 208.

15. Bonsal, *Suitors and Suppliants*, pp 237–8.

16. Fifield, *Woodrow Wilson and the Far East*, p 210. Chu, *V.K. Wellington Koo* (a), p 51, claims the meeting took place on the 24th, and that it was held on a manufactured pretext, that of introducing Wilson to the reformer Liang Qichao and the founder of the Chinese National Socialist Party, Carsun Chang.

17. Fifield, *Woodrow Wilson and the Far East*, p 213.

18. King, *Woodrow Wilson, Wellington Koo*, p 15.

19. King, *Woodrow Wilson, Wellington Koo*, p 16.

20. King, *Woodrow Wilson, Wellington Koo*, p 18.

21. King, *Woodrow Wilson, Wellington Koo*, p 19.

22. King, *Woodrow Wilson, Wellington Koo*, p 20.

23. Bonsal, *Suitors and Suppliants*, p 236.

24. Bonsal, *Suitors and Suppliants*, p 239.

25. Bonsal, *Suitors and Suppliants*, p 241. For biographies of Wilson's China advisers, see Fifield, *Woodrow Wilson and the Far East*, pp 230–1.

6: Days of Sorrow

1. Fifield, *Woodrow Wilson and the Far East*, p 315.

2. Bonsal, *Suitors and Suppliants*, p 243.

3. Chu, *V.K. Wellington Koo* (b), p 28.

4. Chu, *V.K. Wellington Koo* (b), p 29.

5. Pearl, *Morrison of Peking*, p 384, refers to this disparagingly as the 'booby prize' of the Peace Conference. The astronomical instruments can still be seen today, and make for an engaging sight in the

embassy district of Beijing on the rooftop of their
fortified Observatory. See J Clements, *Beijing: The
Biography of a City* (Sutton Publishing, Stroud: 2007)
pp 66–7.

6. Lu, *Ways of Confucius and of Christ*, p 42.
7. Fifield, *Woodrow Wilson and the Far East*, pp 317–19.
8. Fifield, *Woodrow Wilson and the Far East*, pp 321–2.
   Fifield also includes the text of the irate letter written
   but not sent by Reinsch after he discovered how little
   attention had been paid to his advice over Shandong at
   the Peace Conference.
9. King, *Woodrow Wilson, Wellington Koo*, p 25.
10. King, *Woodrow Wilson, Wellington Koo*, p 26.
11. Craft, *V.K. Wellington Koo*, p 59.
12. Lu, *Ways of Confucius and of Christ*, p 42.
13. Fifield, *Woodrow Wilson and the Far East*, pp 334–5.
    Strangely, one of Koo's strongest supporters in the
    arguments was an unlikely ally – Japan's Baron Makino.
14. King, *Woodrow Wilson, Wellington Koo*, p 29.

7: Marriage in Haste

1. Fifield, *Woodrow Wilson and the Far East*, pp 339–40.
2. King, *Woodrow Wilson, Wellington Koo*, p 31.
3. Fifield, *Woodrow Wilson and the Far East*, pp 348–9,
   356–9.
4. *Hui-lan Koo*, p 115.
5. Lu, *Ways of Confucius and of Christ*, p 42.
6. Or so it is stated in *Hui-lan Koo*, p 124; *No Feast Lasts
   Forever*, p 117, implies that the wedding and the opening
   of the League both took place in November *1919* –
   probably an oversight by a ghostwriter attempting
   to make sense of several digressions. Madame Koo

also implies that the engagement ball was given in her honour, which seems unlikely since so many guests did not know who she was. October 10th, however, is 'Double Tenth' day, the anniversary of the Wuchang uprising and the official commencement date of the Chinese Republic, so it seems likely that the engagement was announced at a government occasion.

7. 'A Footnote to the Bab Ballads', *Punch*, Vol 159, 24 November 1920.

8. *No Feast Lasts Forever*, p 127.

9. Chu, *V.K. Wellington Koo* (a), pp 80–2. The full text of the Nine Power Treaty is given in Tung, *Wartime Diplomacy*, pp 141–5.

10. *No Feast Lasts Forever*, p 140. An excerpt from Koo's speech to the students appears on p 121 of Chu, *V.K. Wellington Koo* (a).

11. Chu, *V.K. Wellington Koo* (a), p 133.

12. *Hui-lan Koo*, pp 157–8. With admissions such as this, it is perhaps understandable why Wellington Koo was so keen to prevent his wife publishing her memoirs.

8: China in Chaos

1. Chu, *V.K. Wellington Koo* (a), p 233.

2. Chu, *V.K. Wellington Koo* (a), p 221.

3. Chu, *V.K. Wellington Koo* (a), pp 233–4.

4. Chu, *V.K. Wellington Koo* (b), p 110.

5. *Hui-lan Koo*, pp 251–2; Craft, *V.K. Wellington Koo*, p 82. Madame Koo suspects Japan was behind the incident; Craft lays the blame more persuasively with a pro-Soviet lobby.

6. Chu, *V.K. Wellington Koo* (b), p 120.

7. *Hui-lan Koo*, pp 261–2, claims he fled to Tianjin.

8. S Airlie, *Reginald Johnston, Chinese Mandarin* (National Museums of Scotland, Edinburgh: 2001) pp 80–1.

9. *Hui-lan Koo*, p 275.

10. Tung, *Wartime Diplomacy*, p 94.

11. Craft, *V.K. Wellington Koo*, p 91.

9: The Spreading Whirlpool

1. Craft, *V.K. Wellington Koo*, p 94.

2. Chu, *V.K. Wellington Koo* (b), p 124.

3. Chu, *V.K. Wellington Koo* (b), p 125.

4. Selle, *Donald of China*, p 274.

5. *Hui-lan Koo*, p 319.

6. *Hui-lan Koo*, p 321.

7. Chu, *V.K. Wellington Koo* (b), p 131.

8. Chu, *V.K. Wellington Koo* (b), p 132.

9. Chu, *V.K. Wellington Koo* (b), p 133.

10. Chu, *V.K. Wellington Koo* (b), p 135.

11. Chu, *V.K. Wellington Koo* (b), p 136.

12. *Hui-lan Koo*, p 329.

13. Chu, *V.K. Wellington Koo* (b), p 141.

14. Craft, *V.K. Wellington Koo*, p 109.

10: The Dark Clouds

1. Craft, *V.K. Wellington Koo*, p 117.

2. *Hui-lan Koo*, p 340.

3. Craft, *V.K. Wellington Koo*, p 113.

4. Craft, *V.K. Wellington Koo*, p 118.

5. Craft, *V.K. Wellington Koo*, p 121.

6. Tung, *Wartime Diplomacy*, p 104.

7. Tung, *Wartime Diplomacy*, p 114.

8. Tung, *Wartime Diplomacy*, p 117.

9. Tung, *Wartime Diplomacy*, p 134
10. Craft, *V.K. Wellington Koo*, p 122.
11. Craft, *V.K. Wellington Koo*, p 124.
12. Tung, *Wartime Diplomacy*, p 150.
13. Tung, *Wartime Diplomacy*, p 158.
14. Craft, *V.K. Wellington Koo*, p 127.
15. Craft, *V.K. Wellington Koo*, p 128.
16. Craft, *V.K. Wellington Koo*, p130.
17. *No Feast Lasts Forever*, p 223. Madame Koo refers to her rival as Mrs Goat, likely to be a play on the Chinese *yang*, and the parties' true names, Juliana and Clarence Young.
18. *Hui-lan Koo*, p 396.
19. *Hui-lan Koo*, p 398.
20. *No Feast Lasts Forever*, p 232.
21. Chu, *V.K. Wellington Koo* (b), p 164.
22. Chu, *V.K. Wellington Koo* (b), p 166.

11: The Divided Nations

1. Tung, *Wartime Diplomacy*, p 86.
2. Craft, *Wartime Diplomacy*, p 205.
3. Chu, *V.K. Wellington Koo* (b), p 169.
4. Craft, *V.K. Wellington Koo*, p 229.
5. Chu, *V.K. Wellington Koo* (b), p 174.
6. Chu, *V.K. Wellington Koo* (b), pp 173–4.
7. Craft, *V.K. Wellington Koo*, p 236.
8. Craft, *V.K. Wellington Koo*, p 250.
9. Craft, *V.K. Wellington Koo*, p 251.
10. *No Feast Lasts Forever*, p 290; Tung, *Wartime Diplomacy*, p 96; Chu, *V.K. Wellington Koo* (b), p 175, notes that Koo was forced to resign in the face of pressure from Communist China, but does not

elaborate. Koo's most famous decision as a judge was his minority argument in the case of El Al Flight 402 from Vienna to Tel Aviv, which was shot down by the Bulgarian air force after straying into Bulgarian airspace on 27 July 1955.

11. [Anon], 'Lots of Trouble', *Time*, 26 June 1939.

Chronology

YEAR	AGE	LIFE
1888		29 January: Wellington Koo (Gu Weijun) born in Shanghai.
1891	3	Joins Confucian school of Master Zu (to 1898).
1899	11	Enrolled at Anglo-Japanese Junior College in Shanghai, but withdrawn due to ill-health. 'Bicycle incident'.
1900	12	Enrolled at Talent Fostering School, Shanghai.
1903	15	After a year at US missionary school, departs for the USA: studies at the Cook Academy in Ithaca.
1905	17	Enrols at Columbia University.
1908	20	Awarded BA in Liberal Arts from Columbia. Marries first wife during a vacation in Shanghai: the couple move to America, but are soon divorced. Meets Tang Shaoyi in Washington.
1909	21	Awarded MA in Political Science from Columbia.

YEAR	HISTORY	CULTURE
1888	Kaiser Wilhelm II crowned. Suez Canal convention.	Rudyard Kipling, *Plain Tales from the Hills*.
1891	Triple Alliance (Austria-Hungary, Germany, Italy) renewed for 12 years. Franco-Russian entente.	Thomas Hardy, *Tess of the D'Urbervilles*. Mahler, Symphony No 1.
1899	Outbreak of Second Boer War. First Peace Conference at the Hague.	Rudyard Kipling, *Stalky and Co*. Elgar, 'Enigma Variations'.
1900	Boxer Rebellion: siege of Beijing legations. Second Boer War: relief of Mafeking.	Joseph Conrad, *Lord Jim*. Anton Chekhov, *Uncle Vanya.*.
1903	Beginning of Anglo-French Entente Cordiale. Wright Brothers' first flight.	George Bernard Shaw, *Man and Superman*. Film: *The Great Train Robbery*.
1905	End of Russo-Japanese War.	Edith Wharton, *House of Mirth*.
1908	*The Daily Telegraph* publishes remarks about German hostility towards England made by Kaiser Wilhelm II. William Howard Taft elected US President.	E M Forster, *A Room with a View*. Kenneth Grahame, *The Wind in the Willows*.
1909	Anglo-German discussions on the control of Baghdad railway.	H G Wells, *Tono-Bungay* Matisse, *The Dance*.

YEAR	AGE	LIFE
1912	24	Receives Ph.D from Columbia.
		Leaves Columbia early to become English secretary to Yuan Shikai.
1913	25	Second marriage, to Tang Baoyu, daughter of Tang Shaoyi.
		Becomes assistant to the Foreign Minister, W W Yen, his first diplomatic appointment.
1915	27	Koo Drafts the English-language response to the Japanese 21 Demands from his hospital bed.
		Made Chinese Minister to the United States, Mexico, Cuba and Peru.
1916	28	Birth of Koo's son Dechang. (T C Koo).
		Death of Yuan Shikai; China's republicans split into two factions, ushering in the 'Warlord Era'.
1917	29	Father dies.
		China declares war on Germany.
		Lansing-Ishii Agreement, under which US recognises Japanese rights in Manchuria.
1918	30	Daughter Patricia born.
		Death of wife in influenza pandemic.
		28 September: Duan Qirui's agreement with Japan allows Japanese troops on Shandong railway.

YEAR	HISTORY	CULTURE
1912	*Titanic* sinks. Outbreak of Balkan War. Woodrow Wilson is elected US President.	C G Jung, *The Theory of Psychoanalysis.* Ravel, *Daphnis and Chloe.*
1913	Second Balkan War breaks out.	Thomas Mann, *Death in Venice.*
1915	First World War: Battles of Neuve Chappelle and Loos; Gallipoli campaign.	John Buchan, *The Thirty-Nine Steps.* Film: *The Birth of a Nation.*
1916	First World War: the Battle of the Somme; the Battle of Jutland. US President Woodrow Wilson re-elected.	James Joyce, *Portrait of an Artist as a Young Man.* Richard Strauss, *Ariadne auf Naxos.*
1917	First World War. USA declares war on Germany. German and Russian armistice at Brest-Litovsk. October Revolution.	P G Wodehouse, *The Man With Two Left Feet.* Film: *Easy Street.*
1918	First World War. Treaty of Brest-Litovsk between Russia and the Central Powers. German Spring offensives on Western Front fail. Allied offensives on Western Front. Armistice signed between Allies and Germany.	Gerald Manley Hopkins, *Poems.* Luigi Pirandello, *Six Characters in Search of an Author.* Edvard Munch, *Bathing Man.*

YEAR	AGE	LIFE
1919	31	Paris Peace Conference: Initially third Chinese delegate, but later replaces C T Wang as the deputy of the delegation.
		Shanghai Peace Conference.
		Council of Ten meeting in which China and Japan contest claims for Shandong.
		4 May: Protests in Beijing
		Jun: Treaty of Versailles is signed; China is not a signatory, but signs the later Treaties of Trianon, Neuilly and St Germain.
		25 Jul: Karakhan Manifesto.
		10 Oct: Proposes to Oei Hui-lan.
		Shandong Conference for Commemoration of National Humiliation.
1920	32	14 Nov: Marries Oei Hui-lan in Brussels.
		Inaugural session of the League of Nations in Geneva.
		Appointed Chinese minister to Great Britain (to 1922).
1921	33	Possible date of apocryphal 'soupee, soupee' incident.
		Birth of Wellington Koo Jr.
		October. Presents China's Ten Points at the Washington Conference for Limitation of Armaments, and represents China in negotiations over Shandong. A 15-year settlement is agreed with Japan.
1922	34	Recalled to China and becomes Minister for Foreign Affairs during Lincheng Incident.
1923	35	Birth of Freeman Koo.
		Assassination attempt by poison.
1924	36	Bomb explosion at home.
		Seeks refuge in Weihaiwei during coup in Beijing.

YEAR	HISTORY	CULTURE
1919	Communist Revolt in Berlin. Benito Mussolini founds fascist movement in Italy. US Senate votes against ratification of Versailles Treaty.	Bauhaus movement founded by Walter Gropius. Thomas Hardy, *Collected Poems.* Film: *The Cabinet of Dr Caligari.*
1920	Warren G Harding wins US Presidential election. Bolsheviks win Russian Civil War.	F Scott Fitzgerald, *This Side of Paradise.* Rambert School of Ballet formed.
1921	Irish Free State established. Peace treaty signed between Russia and Germany.	Aldous Huxley, *Chrome Yellow.* D H Lawrence, *Women in Love.* Prokofiev, *The Love for Three Oranges.*
1922	Chanak crisis.	T S Eliot, *The Waste Land.*
1923	French occupy the Ruhr. Adolf Hitler's Beer Hall Putsch.	George Gershwin, *Rhapsody in Blue.*
1924	Death of Lenin. Nazi party wins Reichstag seats for the first time.	E M Forster, *A Passage to India.*

YEAR	AGE	LIFE
1926	38	Made acting Premier of China.
1927	39	Goes into exile for 18 months after fall of government.
1929	41	Visit to Manchuria.
1930	42	Nanjing government lifts arrest warrant . Becomes Minister for Foreign Affairs.
1932	44	Represents China on the Lytton Commission that produces the Lytton Report for the League of Nations on Manchuria.
1933	45	Speech at League of Nations in Geneva on Manchuria followed by Japanese walkout.
1936	48	Appointed Chinese ambassador to France (until 1941): refuses offer to become ambassador to USSR.
1938	50	Rejects second offer to become ambassador to USSR.
1940	52	Leaves France for Lisbon during German invasion: later returns as ambassador to Vichy government.

YEAR	HISTORY	CULTURE
1926	General Strike in Great Britain. Germany is admitted into the League of Nations.	Ernest Hemingway, *The Sun Also Rises*. Film: *The General*.
1927	'Black Friday' in Germany – the economic system collapses.	Virginia Woolf, *To the Lighthouse*. Film: *The Jazz Singer*.
1929	Allies agree to evacuate the Rhineland. The Wall Street Crash	Erich Remarque, *All Quiet on the Western Front*. Noel Coward, *Bittersweet*.
1930	London Naval Treaty. Nazi party in Germany gains 107 seats.	T S Eliot, *Ash Wednesday*. W H Auden, *Poems*.
1932	F D Roosevelt wins US Presidential election.	Aldous Huxley, *Brave New World*. Film: *Grand Hotel*.
1933	Adolf Hitler is appointed Chancellor of Germany.	George Orwell, *Down and Out in Paris and London*. Film: *King Kong*.
1936	German troops reoccupy Rhineland. Outbreak of Spanish Civil War. Rome-Berlin Axis proclaimed.	Penguin Books starts paperback revolution. Berlin Olympics. Film: *Modern Times*.
1938	German Anschluss with Austria.	Graham Greene, *Brighton Rock*. Film: *The Adventures of Robin Hood*.
1940	Second World War: German victories in the West. Roosevelt is elected for an unprecedented third term as US president.	Eugene O'Neill, *Long Days Journey into Night*. Films: *The Great Dictator*, *Rebecca*.

YEAR	AGE	LIFE
1941	53	Appointed Chinese ambassador to Great Britain.
1944	56	Represents China on the War Crimes Commission in London.
1945	57	Chinese delegate to the San Francisco Conference for the Establishment of the United Nations.
1946	58	Appointed Chinese ambassador to the United States and Mexico (to 1956). Member of the Far Eastern Commission on Japan (to 1949).
1949	61	Awarded Alexander Hamilton medal. PRC assumes control of all of China except the south-west; ROC retreats to Taiwan.
1952	64	Peace Treaty between China and Japan.
1956	68	Retires from the diplomatic service. Formally divorced from Oei Hui-Lan. Becomes judge at the International Court of Justice.

YEAR	HISTORY	CULTURE
1941	Second World War: Germany invades USSR. Japan attacks Pearl Harbor. Germany and Italy declare war on the USA.	Bertold Brecht, *Mother Courage and Her Children*. Films: *Citizen Kane. The Maltese Falcon.*
1944	Second World War: D-Day landings in France. Claus von Stauffenberg's bomb at Rastenburg fails to kill Hitler.	Tennessee Williams, *The Glass Menagerie*. Film: *Double Indemnity. Henry V.*
1945	Second World War: VE Day, 8 May. USA drops atomic bombs on Hiroshima and Nagasaki. Japan surrenders to Allies.	Benjamin Britten, *Peter Grimes*. Evelyn Waugh, *Brideshead Revisited*. Film: *Brief Encounter*.
1946	UN General Assembly opens in London. Churchill's 'Iron Curtain' speech. Nuremberg establishes guilty verdicts for war crimes.	Bertrand Russell, *History of Western Philosophy*. Film: *Great Expectations*.
1949	Foundation of North Atlantic Treaty Organisation (NATO). USSR tests its first atomic bomb.	Simone de Beauvoir, *The Second Sex*. Film: *The Third Man*.
1952	Death of King George VI: succeeded by Elizabeth II. Mau-Mau Rising in Kenya.	Dylan Thomas, *Collected Poems*. Film: *High Noon*.
1956	Treaty of Rome establishes the European Economic Community (EEC).	Jack Kerouac, *On the Road*. Film: *The Bridge on the River Kwai*.

YEAR	AGE	LIFE
1967	79	Retires as judge, and moves to New York City.
		ROC's seat on UN Security Council given to the PRC.
1985	97	Dies in New York.

YEAR	HISTORY	CULTURE
1967	Six Day War between Israel and Arab States.	The Beatles, *Sgt. Pepper's Lonely Hearts Club Band.*
1985	Major famine in Ethiopia.	Live Aid rock concert for famine relief.

Further Reading

Many memoirs by Chinese Republican diplomats end before the Republic truly got underway – during the 1920s and 1930s, figures were coy about disclosing their allegiances when China's government was in such a state of flux. Koo remained similarly taciturn regarding his own life, writing in a letter to Chu Pao-chin in 1966 that ... *many of my erstwhile official colleagues are still living, and I would not want to lend myself possibly to their embarrassment and cause controversies.* This is particularly relevant in the case of the Paris Peace Conference, for which Koo and other delegates, particularly C T Wang, seem prepared to gloss over their rivalries in later interviews in the interests of presenting a united front. The historian must thus exercise a certain degree of caution, even when dealing with supposedly primary sources.

Koo's papers are held at his alma mater, Columbia University, whose East Asian Institute's Chinese Oral History Project also has a selection of recordings of his reminiscences, transcripts of which fill some 11,000 typewritten pages and eight volumes, the second of which includes his memories of the Peace Conference. Many of these, combined with direct interviews, are put to use in Chu Pao-chin's Ph.D and subsequent book *V.K. Wellington Koo*, which takes his life story up to retirement. Another Koo scholar, Stephen G Craft, is the author of the more recent *V.K. Wellington Koo and the Emergence of Modern China*, which follows Koo's involvement through the dawn of the Communist era and the flight of the Republicans to Taiwan. Chu is largely supportive of Koo, whereas Craft, while still admiring, includes more critical commentary from others. William Tung's *V.K. Wellington Koo and China's Wartime Diplomacy* also makes use of the reminiscence files, although half its page count is given up to reprinting Koo's landmark speeches and addresses.

The *Wunsz King Collection of V.K. Wellington Koo Papers* – compiled by Koo's Paris secretary – details the minutes of meetings between the Chinese diplomats and other powers. Another useful source is the *Waijiao Gongbao* (*Foreign Affairs Gazette*), published by the Republicans in Beijing from 1921–8, and including minutes and annotations on many of Koo's negotiations.

Koo enjoyed such longevity in his career because he avoided factions – he chose diplomacy over politics, and thereby survived many changes in administration while many of his colleagues became associated with rising, and then falling, administrations. Perhaps because of the need for impartiality, Koo's reticence continued during his post-diplomatic legal career. His third wife, Hui-lan, is the primary source about his private life, thanks to her charmingly catty memoirs. A dazzled fiancée at the Peace Conference, and a colourful companion during Koo's ambassadorial days, Madame Koo kept her title after the couple were divorced in 1956, and remained an imposing matriarch of the Koo family, both toward her own children and her step-children. The first version of her memoirs, a 421-page book called simply *Hui-lan Koo*, was printed but withdrawn from publication at her estranged husband's insistence, shortly before it was due to go on sale in 1943. A heavily revised version, assembled with a second collaborator, finally reached the public in 1975 as *No Feast Lasts Forever*, and contained details of an additional 30 years, yet is still 100 pages shorter. There is much in the 1943 book to recommend it, and it remains so tantalisingly obscure that several authorities who should know better have merrily quoted from it without due recognition. However, Madame Koo's memoirs do suffer from occasional lapses, some of which could stem from her use of ghostwriters unfamiliar with China. For example, her first biography gives Wellington Koo's birthdate as 1887, a rookie error one might expect from an amanuensis unfamiliar with the Chinese calendar, but not from a man's wife! Others push her personal agenda – she paints herself as a wide-eyed teenage debutante at the Paris Peace Conference, whereas Craft alludes to her instead as a brassy divorcée whose short-lived first marriage had been swept under the carpet. Unsupported online sources also suggest that she may have been some six or seven years older than she claimed, but as even Wellington Koo might concede, it is ungentlemanly to expect a lady to give her real age. Madame Koo also insists that she is Wellington's 'true' wife, and that Juliana Young, whom Koo introduced publicly as his spouse from the late 1950s onwards, and who was named as such in many of his obituaries in 1985, was no more than an 'imposter'.

Lu Zhengxiang, Koo's supposed superior at the Paris Peace Conference, did not write his memoirs, but did discuss his life and diplomatic career in 40 pages of his *Souvenirs & Pensées*, a collection of reminiscences otherwise weighted towards his later vocation as a Catholic monk; the book was translated as *Ways of Confucius and of Christ*. The best objective analysis of his life is Keegan's in *Diplomacy and Statecraft*. Russell Fifield's *Woodrow Wilson and the Far East* concentrates entirely on Shandong and the discussions surrounding it during the Paris Peace Conference, and hence features much information on Koo, some of it derived directly from interviews, although some appear self-serving – Fifield faithfully repeats Koo's assertion, for example, that he was ignorant of China's 'secret agreements' before he reached Paris, which seems unlikely since he personally drafted some of them. Since the Paris Peace Conference and its after-effects are a *Rashomon* of contending views and vantage points, it is also worth noting that the perspective on Japanese diplomacy in this book is based entirely on the negative impressions of the Chinese. Not all the Japanese were conniving militarists, as demonstrated in the *Makers of the Modern World* study of Koo's supposed adversary at Paris, Prince Saionji Kinmochi. Had circumstances been different, he and Koo might even have been friends.

Airlie, S, *Reginald Johnston, Chinese Mandarin* (National Museums of Scotland, Edinburgh: 2001).

[Anon], 'Mrs Koo Explains Withdrawal of Book', *New York Times*, 27 April 1943.

[Anon], 'Lots of Trouble', *Time*, 26 June 1939.

[Anon], 'The Younger Generation', *Time*, 7 July 1947.

Beasley, W, *Japanese Imperialism 1894–1945* (Clarendon Press, Oxford: 1991).

Bonsal, S, *Suitors and Suppliants: The Little Nations at Versailles* (Prentice Hall, New York: 1946).

Chu, P, *V.K. Wellington Koo: A Study of the Diplomat and Diplomacy of Warlord China, During His Early*

Career, 1919–1924. Doctoral dissertation, University of Pennsylvania, 1971. (Listed as 'Chu, *V.K. Wellington Koo* (a)' in the notes.)

——, *V.K. Wellington Koo: A Case Study of China's Diplomat and Diplomacy of Nationalism 1912–1966* (Chinese University Press, Hong Kong: 1981). (Listed as 'Chu, *V.K. Wellington Koo* '(b)' in the notes.)

Clemenceau, G, *Grandeur and Misery of Victory* (George Harrap, London: 1930).

Clements, J, *Beijing: The Biography of a City* (Sutton Publishing, Stroud: 2007).

——, *Makers of the Modern World – Saionji Kinmochi, Japan* (Haus Publishing, London: 2008).

——, *Mao Zedong* (Haus Publishing, London: 2006).

Craft, S, *V.K. Wellington Koo and the Emergence of Modern China* (University Press of Kentucky, Lexington: 2004).

Encyclopaedia Britannica, DVD-ROM Edition (2002).

Fifield, R, *Woodrow Wilson and the Far East: The Diplomacy of the Shantung Question* (Thomas Y Crowell Company, New York: 1952).

Harada, K, *Fragile Victory: Prince Saionji and the 1930 London Treaty Issue from the Memoirs of Baron Harada Kumao* (Wayne State University Press, Detroit: 1968).

Keegan, N, 'From Chancery to Cloister: The Chinese Diplomat Who Became a Benedictine Monk,' in *Diplomacy and Statecraft*, Vol 10, No 1 (March 1999) pp 177–85.

King, W, *Woodrow Wilson, Wellington Koo and the China Question at the Paris Peace Conference* (A W Sythoff, Leyden: 1959).

Koo, Madame Wellington [Hui-lan], with Mary van Rensselaer Thayer, *Hui-lan Koo: An Autobiography* (Dial Press, New York: 1943).

——, with Isabella Taves, *No Feast Lasts Forever* (Quadrangle Books, New York: 1975).

Koo, V, *The Status of Aliens in China* (Columbia University, New York: 1912).

Lai, H, 'The Chinese-Marxist Left, Chinese students and scholars in America, and the New China: mid-1940s to mid-1950s', in *Chinese America: History and Perspectives*, 1 January 2004 (online).

Lou, T [Lu Zhengxiang], *Souvenirs & Pensées: Lettre à Mes Amis de Grande-Bretagne et D'Amerique* (Dominique Martin Morin, Paris: 1993).

——, *Ways of Confucius and of Christ* (Burns Oates, London: 1948).

Macmillan, M, *Paris 1919* (Random House, New York: 2001).

Pearl, C, *Morrison of Peking* (Penguin Australia, Victoria: 1970).

Selle, E, *Donald of China* (Harper and Brothers, New York: 1948).

Sharp, A, *The Versailles Settlement: Peacemaking in Paris, 1919* (Palgrave, Houndmills: 1991).

Tung, W, *V K. Wellington Koo and China's Wartime Diplomacy* (Center of Asian Studies, St John's University, New York: 1977).

Picture Sources

The author and publishers wish to express their thanks to the following sources of illustrative material and/or permission to reproduce it. They will make proper acknowledgements in future editions in the event that any omissions have occurred.

Topham Picturepoint: pp. 8, 52, 108.

Endpapers
The Signing of Peace in the Hall of Mirrors, Versailles, 28th June 1919 by Sir William Orpen (Bridgeman Art Library)
Front row: Dr Johannes Bell (Germany) signing with Herr Hermann Müller leaning over him
Middle row (seated, left to right): General Tasker H Bliss, Col E M House, Mr Henry White, Mr Robert Lansing, President Woodrow Wilson (United States); M Georges Clemenceau (France); Mr David Lloyd George, Mr Andrew Bonar Law, Mr Arthur J Balfour, Viscount Milner, Mr G N Barnes (Great Britain); Prince Saionji (Japan)
Back row (left to right): M Eleftherios Venizelos (Greece); Dr Afonso Costa (Portugal); Lord Riddell (British Press);

Sir George E Foster (Canada); M Nikola Pašić (Serbia);
M Stephen Pichon (France); Col Sir Maurice Hankey,
Mr Edwin S Montagu (Great Britain); the Maharajah of
Bikaner (India); Signor Vittorio Emanuele Orlando (Italy);
M Paul Hymans (Belgium); General Louis Botha (South
Africa); Mr W M Hughes (Australia)

Jacket images

(Front): Getty Images.
(Back): *Peace Conference at the Quai d'Orsay* by Sir
William Orpen (akg Images).
Left to right (seated): Signor Orlando (Italy); Mr Robert
Lansing, President Woodrow Wilson (United States); M
Georges Clemenceau (France); Mr David Lloyd George, Mr
Andrew Bonar Law, Mr Arthur J Balfour (Great Britain);
Left to right (standing): M Paul Hymans (Belgium); Mr
Eleftherios Venizelos (Greece); The Emir Feisal (The
Hashemite Kingdom); Mr W F Massey (New Zealand);
General Jan Smuts (South Africa); Col E M House (United
States); General Louis Botha (South Africa); Prince Saionji
(Japan); Mr W M Hughes (Australia); Sir Robert Borden
(Canada); Mr G N Barnes (Great Britain); M Ignacy
Paderewski (Poland)

Index

Makers of the Modern World

UK PUBLICATION: November 2008 to December 2010
CLASSIFICATION: Biography/History/
    International Relations
FORMAT: 198 × 128mm
EXTENT: 208pp
ILLUSTRATIONS: 6 photographs plus 4 maps
TERRITORY: world

Chronology of life in context, full index, bibliography innovative layout
with sidebars